LIFE AFTER SUICIDE

ALSO BY JENNIFER ASHTON, M.D.

*Your Body Beautiful: Clockstopping Secrets to
Staying Healthy, Strong, and Sexy in Your 30s, 40s,
and Beyond*

*Eat This, Not That! When You're Expecting: The
Doctor-Recommended Plan for Baby and You!*

*The Body Scoop for Girls: A Straight-Talk Guide to a
Healthy, Beautiful You*

LIFE AFTER SUICIDE

FINDING
COURAGE, COMFORT & COMMUNITY
AFTER UNTHINKABLE LOSS

JENNIFER ASHTON, M.D.

wm WILLIAM MORROW
An Imprint of HarperCollins*Publishers*

LIFE AFTER SUICIDE. Copyright © 2019 by Jennifer Ashton. All rights re-served. Printed in the United States of America. No part of this book may be used or reproduced in any manner whatsoever without written permis-sion except in the case of brief quotations embodied in critical articles and reviews. For information, address HarperCollins Publishers, 195 Broad-way, New York, NY 10007.

HarperCollins books may be purchased for educational, business, or sales promotional use. For information, please email the Special Markets De-partment at SPsales@harpercollins.com.

FIRST EDITION

DESIGNED BY WILLIAM RUOTO

Library of Congress Cataloging-in-Publication Data has been applied for.

ISBN 978-0-06-290603-8

19 20 21 22 23 LSC 10 9 8 7 6 5 4 3 2 1

To Alex and Chloe,
and to Dr. Rob Ashton,
who created them with me
and adored them as much as I do.

A portion of the proceeds from this book will be donated to Vibrant Emotional Health, which administers the National Suicide Prevention Lifeline and other programs related to crisis response and emotional well-being.

Dr. Jennifer Ashton is donating a portion of the proceeds from the sale of *Life After Suicide* to the American Foundation for Suicide Prevention in honor of Dr. Robert Ashton, Jr.

CONTENTS

LIFE AFTER SUICIDE

*L*IFE AFTER SUICIDE IS A BOOK I COULD NEVER HAVE IMAGINED writing, let alone from personal experience. It's taken me a year and a half to be able to offer a book that's focused on the *life* part of the title rather than the suicide, a book about my family's journey toward healing after a sudden, devastating tragedy and, I'm eternally grateful to add, a book about other suicide survivors' journeys as well. This is a book about hope, and strength, and resilience, and growth, and how, with a lot of help and love, we found our way out of a darkness I was sometimes afraid might swallow us whole.

The national headlines read "Surgeon Jumps to His Death After Divorce from TV Personality Wife." The "Surgeon" was Dr. Robert Ashton, a brilliant thoracic specialist. I'm the "TV Personality Wife," Dr. Jennifer Ashton, ABC News Chief Medical Correspondent, a regular guest health expert on *Good Morning America*, *Dr. Oz*, and *The Doctors*, a doctor married to a doctor for twenty-one years, and proud mother of Alex and Chloe, the two greatest teenage children in the history of teenage children. Our family was immune from suicide . . . until we weren't, until we found

out the hard way that suicide is an equal-opportunity horror that strikes families regardless of race, color, religion,
age, education, occupation, achievements, or socioeconomic
status. Or, to put it in a simple medical analogy I've come
to use, all tushes are the same when they're hanging out the
back of a hospital gown.

Obviously, in order to share all the steps and missteps of
our journey, and the journeys of the other suicide survivors
who were generous enough to share theirs as well, I had to
relive the past year and a half that started with a detective
showing up in our living room to tell me about a note that
was found on Rob's "remains." Writing this book has been
a cathartic, revealing, therapeutic, scary, often excruciating
exercise, but it will have been worth it if it leads even one
of you to believe in that light at the end of a tunnel of despair I felt so lost in myself.

I hadn't fully realized until I looked back how far my
kids and I have come, and how much we've learned about
ourselves and the world around us, since the day Rob took
his life. I'm embarrassed to say, as a doctor, that I knew
nothing about suicide and the stigma that surrounds it
until I found myself feeling self-conscious, even ashamed,
that my husband, my children's father, killed himself. Since
childhood I've had a hardwired aversion to weakness, vulnerability, failure, insecurity, blame, fear, and flaws; but
suddenly I was hit squarely in the face with each and every
one of those qualities—not in Rob, but in myself. For a

long time my impulse was to bury them, so that I could put up a strong front for Alex and Chloe; and because I'm inherently private, it felt more comfortable to stay busy, appear as normal as possible, and, as best I could, hide the fact that I was shattered and struggling to put myself back together. There were two people with whom I shared everything I was thinking and feeling. Otherwise, exposing myself, my imperfections, and my family's challenges in the wake of Rob's suicide, especially to millions of television viewers, seemed much too scary.

It took a while, and a lot of trial-and-error learning—what helps and what doesn't, who your real friends are and who they're not, what to expect and not expect when inevitable milestones come along, what to expect and not expect of yourself and those around you—before I tentatively started reaching out to a handful of other suicide survivors, essentially to ask how they were getting through the recovery and healing process. I was hoping for words of wisdom and advice. What I got was so much more than that. I discovered that there's a huge community of incredible, heroic suicide survivors, sadly growing by the day as suicide reaches epidemic proportions, who are more than willing to say to hell with the stigma, tell their stories, and open their hearts and their arms; and it was more empowering than I can describe to hear them say, and mean, "I know exactly what you're feeling, and you're not alone."

Then, a year and four months after Rob took his life,

another devastating suicide hit the news; and as a result of my televised interview about it, and the overwhelming reaction to the interview, I was given the opportunity to learn another life-changing lesson: as empowering as it is to hear someone say and mean, "I know exactly how you're feeling, and you're not alone," it's even more empowering to come out of hiding, flaws and all, and say exactly the same thing to others who need it.

If you're one of those who needs it, or if you know and love someone who does, this book is for you. I'm still learning. I still have days when this all seems surreal. I still wonder sometimes if I'll ever feel unbroken again, and I can't pretend that this whole hard journey is behind me once and for all. But I've come far enough to reach out to you in these pages and promise, as part of an extraordinary community of survivors whose stories you're about to read, that there really is life after suicide.

I T WAS SATURDAY, FEBRUARY 11, 2017.

I got up at around 6:00 A.M. Thanks to my regular appearances on ABC's *Good Morning America*, I'm programmed to be an early riser. Six A.M. is sleeping in for me.

My sweet seventeen-year-old daughter, Chloe, was an hour and a half away at the Lawrenceville private boarding school and a proud member of their varsity ice hockey team. My wonderful eighteen-year-old son, Alex, was a freshman at Columbia University, but he'd been home for a couple of days recovering from the flu. As I walked past his closed bedroom door I felt a wave of relief that he'd chosen a college so close by and could come home when and if he needed to. I paused at his door to listen for a second. It was silent inside. He was obviously sound asleep, and I smiled at what a still, peaceful sleeper he is as I quietly kept walking.

Our apartment was on the fortieth floor of a doorman building in Fort Lee, New Jersey, with an incredible view of the New York skyline across the river and the George Washington Bridge about three hundred yards from our building's entrance. I headed to the living room window to watch some scattered clouds pass over Manhattan and formulate my game plan for the day. I'm hardwired to open my eyes every morning thinking, "How much can I get done today? How much can I accomplish, and how soon can I start?" For better or worse, the word *leisurely* is not in my vocabulary, and weekends are no exception.

I quickly decided to stick with my usual Saturday routine—an 8:30 A.M. spin class at SoulCycle in the city, just fifteen minutes away on the Upper West Side, for my daily health fix, then home for a shower and to launch the rest of the day from there.

I happened to glance at the clock as I drove across the George Washington Bridge: 8:13. I was cutting it close; but I managed to make it to SoulCycle with a couple of minutes to spare, choose a bike in the back row as spin class got under way, and let my body take over so my mind could wander into the uncharted territory my life had become.

Eighteen days earlier, on January 23, I'd been in a courtroom with my husband, a brilliant thoracic surgeon named Dr. Robert Ashton, Jr., finalizing our divorce. We hugged each other and cried when we left that courtroom, and we hugged again when he walked me to my car. We'd tried for more than a year to salvage our twenty-one-year marriage, with the help of family therapist Dr. Sue Simring. But finally one day, at the end of a session, she said out loud what I'm sure we already knew:

"The only thing you two have in common anymore is your children. Your differences are irreconcilable, and I would have no clue where to start if you told me you wanted to stay together and make this marriage work. I think you should call your lawyers."

She gave us a moment to take that in and then added, "I want you to know, you're welcome to keep seeing me, either as a couple or individually."

I'm a big believer in leaping at every opportunity to work on myself. After all, plenty to work on! "Yes," I said. "Absolutely. Thank you." And I kept right on seeing her.

Rob, on the other hand, shrugged off the invitation with a simple, polite, "Nope, I'm good."

I wasn't surprised. I'd been the one to bring up the subject of couples therapy, and then divorce, in the first place, and not once had he said anything resembling, "No! I love you! Please don't do this!" His reaction, or lack of one, kind of capsulized what our relationship had evolved into—no highs, no lows, less a couple than just two very busy people living their own very busy lives, sharing a home because that's where our children were, but little if anything more.

Following Dr. Simring's advice, we'd sat down together from the beginning to tell Alex and Chloe that we were in couples therapy. The next day Chloe went with me to Los Angeles, where I was shooting an episode of *The Doctors*; and that night, in bed, in our hotel room, lying there in the darkness, she quietly announced, "Mom, I need you to know, if you and Dad can't work things out, Alex and I don't ever want you to stay together for our sake."

I can't begin to count the number of times my kids have blown me away. That was one of those times.

A few months later, using the language Dr. Simring had given us after that final pronouncement in her office, we sat down with our children again.

"Your mom and I love each other," Rob told them, "and of course we love you. But we don't love each other anymore in the way that a husband and wife need to love each other, the kind of love that can sustain a marriage. So we've decided it will be best for all of us if we live separately and get a divorce."

I started to cry and choked out the words, "I'm so sorry. We know this is upsetting for you. We really tried."

Alex, a teenager and all boy, almost cut me off in his race to the top of his priority list. "Where are the dogs going to live?"

It was such an Alex thing to say that it made us smile as I explained that the two big dogs—our Labs, Nigel and Remy—would go with Dad, and the little one, Mason the Morkie, whom I'd just brought home seven months earlier, would stay with us.

"Where's Dad going to live?"

"Right across the street."

It had been a mutual decision between Rob and me that he find an apartment close to ours. Just because our marriage was ending didn't mean we wanted to be as far away from each other as possible, and we weren't about to let this divorce separate our children from either of their parents.

We looked at Chloe to see how she was doing with all this. She was doing fine. "You know," she said, "you two haven't acted like a married couple for a long time, so it won't really be that different."

And it wasn't, any more than the divorce proceedings were that different from our marriage—no nastiness, no drama, no vindictive battles, no below-the-belt accusations, making sure every step of the way to treat each other, and our marriage, with the respect we and our twenty-one years together deserved. It was important to us to have what we called an "evolved divorce." We didn't see any need for the all-too-common *War of the Roses* that so many couples devolve into. We still loved each other. We still cared deeply about each other. We just didn't want to be married to each other anymore. Above all, we wanted to show our children that divorce doesn't have to be ugly and vitriolic. We could, and would, do it differently, and do it better.

So there I was, pedaling away at SoulCycle, about to turn forty-eight and single again for the first time in more than two decades. I felt optimistic, and sad, and confident, and uncertain, thinking about dating, thinking about not dating, trying to imagine what my life would look like in a couple of years when both my children would be in college and starting lives of their own. And I hated it, but I was also wrestling with a feeling that was completely unfamiliar to me, something I'd been struggling with and working on in therapy—with the end of my marriage came a feeling of failure.

I came up with the idea of perfection as a game plan when I was five years old, my strategy for getting through my parents' first divorce. (They ended up remarrying and then divorcing again when I was twenty-two.) When my father moved out of the house, I decided that if I did whatever it took to become as perfect as possible, he'd be proud of me, he'd always love me, and he'd never, ever leave me. That should work, right? (Mind you, it took a lot of therapy to figure that out. At the age of five it was pure instinct on my part.)

Not only did it work, since my dad, my mom, and my younger brother, Evan, and I have always been and always will be close, but that coping mechanism ended up serving me beautifully. From that very early age it became second nature to set high standards for myself and work hard to achieve them, with the result that I became accustomed to being successful at pretty much every challenge I took on.

After graduating as an art history major from Columbia College, Columbia University, I completed a post-baccalaureate premedical program, also at Columbia. In my third and final year I was doing research in a Columbia lab in cardiovascular pharmacology when I was introduced to a handsome, charismatic, friendly surgeon named Robert

Ashton. I was twenty-five. He was just turning thirty, doing a year of research during his general surgery residency in the lab of his good friend and mentor, Dr. Mehmet Oz.

Rob didn't just ask me out. In a first for me, he asked me out for two nights in a row. "What are you doing Friday and Saturday night?" It worked. All over the place. We were engaged ten weeks later. He enjoyed telling people, "If I hadn't known I was going to marry her, there wouldn't have been a second date."

Our courtship was a really beautiful love story, and we got married the following year. It felt like my dream destiny. My dad was a New York cardiologist. My mom was a registered nurse. My brother, Evan, was applying to medical school and would soon be on his way to becoming Chief of Reconstructive and Plastic Surgery at the Montefiore Medical Center in the Bronx. I was studying to be a doctor and marrying a doctor. Perfection was getting more perfect by the minute.

I started med school at Columbia three months after we got married, while Rob continued his residency in Pittsburgh. Two years into our marriage we decided to start a family. In keeping with my insistence on mastering the task at hand, I was pregnant a month later. I spent my first pregnancy flying back and forth to Pittsburgh to see Rob; and then, two weeks before our son was born, Rob moved back to New York to start his fellowship in Cardiothoracic Surgery at Columbia. I took eight weeks off after giving birth to Alex, and seventeen months later Rob and I had the joy of introducing Alex to his beautiful little sister, Chloe.

In the meantime, I was still almost making a game of proving to myself that I really could have it all and do it all. I was elected president of my medical school class four years in a row. Despite commuting back and forth to Pittsburgh for the first several months of my marriage, having two babies, and taking three months off, I graduated right on time, in the top 20 percent of my class. Upon graduation, I was awarded the prestigious Herbert Bartlestone Award for Excellence in Pharmacology. Then, after my residency in Ob-Gyn in New York City, I built a successful private practice that eventually grew to more than three thousand patients. Several years later, without missing a beat in my private practice, I began making television appearances as a medical correspondent. One week after my first appearance on-air, I was offered a TV contract with the Fox News Channel, which led to network news contracts with CBS News and, in 2012, the number-one-rated ABC News Network. I was seen regularly on such shows as *Good Morning America, Dr. Oz,* and *The Doctors.* I authored and coauthored a few books on women's health and nutrition; and in my nonexistent spare time, I picked up a master's degree in Nutrition and became Board-certified in Obesity Medicine. I never neglected my exercise obsession, competing in a few triathlons, doing a seventy-mile bike race in Colorado with Rob, and working out both at SoulCycle and at the gym in our apartment building with my personal trainer, Cliff. And yes, thank you for asking, I occasionally indulged in recreational scuba diving and had four PADI (Professional Association of Diving Instructors) scuba certifications. I also happened to be, of course, a proud, actively involved wife and mother, with a successful thoracic surgeon husband, an absolutely gorgeous family, and a million pictures to prove it.

In other words, I was, in reality, Wonder Woman. Hear me roar. Look up "Type-A Overachiever" in any psychology book and there I'll be, smiling back at you. I loved every minute of it. It was a joy, not a burden, living up to my own incredibly high expectations. On paper I even kind of envied myself.

But now, imagery and public perception aside, there was no way around it, my marriage was over. The divorce was final. It was no one's fault, and it didn't matter how hard Rob and I worked to try to fix it, or how amicably we'd handled things. The bottom line was, somehow or another, I'd failed. I knew it, my children knew it, my family knew it, our friends knew it, and soon everyone else would know it too. I wished I didn't care what everyone else knew, and thought, and felt about it. But I did.

I had a lot of work to do.

At the same time, I couldn't let myself lose sight of all I had to be grateful for. Our children had come through the divorce really well, because, thanks to Dr. Simring, Rob and I had handled it really well. Rob had given up his surgical career rather abruptly in 2012 and transitioned to a career in biotech/medical businesses, which seemed to make him happy. Socially, he'd started dating a few months earlier, he was exercising regularly, taking good care of himself. . . .

Although he'd sounded awful when I called him on Tuesday about a minor health insurance thing. I asked him if he was okay, and he explained it away with, "Yeah, it's just things going on at work." And Wednesday night Mom and I had met him at Chloe's ice hockey game, the last home game of the season. We took family photos and sat together at dinner at the rink after the game, when Chloe presented him with a white Lawrenceville hat he'd been wanting for months. He seemed to be enjoying himself, but when Mom and I were alone in the car on the way home I mentioned that I didn't think he looked very good. Mom didn't think so either.

On the other hand, he'd texted on both Thursday and Friday to ask how Alex was doing with this bout of the flu, adding, "I'm at work, but let me know if you need anything. I can leave." I thanked him and assured him it wasn't necessary. We had plenty of Tamiflu and food on hand, I was going to be around all day, and I'd keep him posted on our son.

Obviously Rob was okay. Nothing to worry about. And

yet another reminder that, divorce or no divorce, he and I would always, *always* put our kids first, and always easily work together when it came to making sure they'd have whatever they needed. I was so grateful.

In fact, I had a lot to be grateful for, and I needed to stay focused on counting my blessings. Alex and Chloe were great. My life's work, devoted to women's health and to helping people in general, was great. My parents, my brother, my colleagues, my staff, my patients, and my friends were great. With their help and support, and Dr. Simring's, I was going to be great too. Physically, mentally, and financially, I was strong and healthy, and I knew how to take care of myself. I was fortunate enough to have two great careers that gave me financial independence. Whatever this new chapter in my life had in store for me, I could handle it, because that was my self-programmed default. I could do this, and do it well.

By the time spin class ended I was reenergized and looking forward to the future; and I left SoulCycle headed for home, ready to attack the rest of my day. I had no idea, not even the slightest twinge of a premonition, that it would be months before I could bring myself to go back there again.

I WAS STEPPING OUT OF THE SHOWER, SHORTLY BEFORE 10:00 A.M., when the phone rang. I answered it to hear the familiar voice of the building's doorman.

"Dr. Ashton," he said, "there are three detectives on their way up to your apartment."

Three detectives? What? I froze. What could detectives possibly want with me? I'm a rule follower. I don't do trouble, let alone trouble with law enforcement. Just the thought of it horrifies me. This was obviously some kind of mistake. I hadn't done anything.

Oh. Except . . .

I'd been out to dinner the night before with Lisa Oz. Lisa and her husband, Dr. Mehmet Oz, had been close friends of Rob's and mine for more than twenty years, so close that I'm the godmother of one of their children, and Lisa is my son's godmother. We'd had a quiet, relaxing meal together; but then, on the way home, out of carelessness or exhaustion or too much on my mind or whatever, no excuses, I made an illegal U-turn. I got pulled over, I got a ticket, I deserved it, end of story. And now a team of detectives was coming to my door. Seriously? Since when did the Fort Lee PD have so much time on their hands that they sent detectives to follow up on a traffic ticket? This was ridiculous.

The doorbell rang. I took a deep breath and walked, almost marched, to answer it, hoping it hadn't woken my son.

The three plainclothes detectives at the door looked grim and unfriendly. I'm sure I did too.

"Dr. Jennifer Ashton?" one of them asked.

"Yes. What's the problem?"

Rather than answer my perfectly reasonable question, they showed me their badges, while the apparent spokesman of the group explained, "We're from the Port Authority Police, and we need to talk to you, ma'am. Let's go inside and sit down."

Just when I thought I couldn't get more confused—the Port Authority Police? In charge of tunnels, bridges, bus terminals . . . *What?*

"What's the problem?" I repeated. "What's this about?"

Still no answer, just a firm, "Ma'am, you really need to come inside with us and sit down."

I led them into the living room, my anxiety building with every step, and perched on the edge of the nearest chair, while Detective Spokesman took a seat on the ottoman in front of me, no more than a foot away. I'd given up on asking him questions, so I just silently stared at him.

He cut right to the chase.

"Dr. Ashton, we found a piece of paper with your name and number and the words 'call my wife' on the remains of your husband."

I'd already fallen to my knees and collapsed onto him on the word *remains*. I was instantly beyond shock, hysterical, unable to process it, unable to do or say anything beyond screaming, "No!" over and over and over again.

Next thing I knew Alex was racing in from his bedroom and kneeling beside me. For some reason he assumed something terrible had happened to my father.

"Mom, is it Grandpa?"

I grabbed him, suddenly consumed with the thought, "Oh, my God, my poor Alex!" I wrapped my arms around him, held on tight, and sobbed, "Alex, it's Daddy! It's Daddy!"

The detective still had the rest of his job to do. He kept his voice calm and compounded the horror as he answered a question I hadn't even thought to ask yet.

"It appears that at approximately 8:34 this morning, Dr. Ashton jumped from the George Washington Bridge and took his own life. His body was recovered at Hazard's Dock shortly after he jumped, with the note in his pocket about contacting you."

I went numb. How do you comprehend the incomprehensible? Rob hadn't just died. He'd killed himself. I remember as if it happened yesterday the sensation of being slammed all at once with a hundred disjointed fragments of thoughts.

The George Washington Bridge. Half of our apartment looked out on that bridge. Rob knew Alex was home with me. He knew I'd be wide awake at that hour. What if one or both of us had been looking out the window when he jumped? Then again, if he was determined to end his life, he would never, ever have chosen a way that might have led to Alex or Chloe or me finding him.

I'd been driving across that bridge at 8:13. Twenty-one minutes before he killed himself. What if I'd driven past him as he walked toward the bridge and hadn't stopped? What if I'd come upon him at the very moment he was climbing onto a railing, too late to pull him back, and seen him disappear? It still haunts me.

While I was at SoulCycle, focused on spin class and the rest of my life, Rob was all alone, ending his. It was unfathomable to me. I don't have formal training as a psychologist, but every doctor knows the classic signs of depression. Rob had none of them. Dr. Simring had even asked us in therapy one day if we would ever consider taking our own life. My answer was, "No." Rob's was, "Absolutely not."

I was still holding my son, overwhelmed by more thoughts than I could begin to take in, when the detective who'd broken the news to me handed me a business card, with an invitation to call if there was anything we needed. He joined his colleagues, the three of them told us they were very sorry for our loss, and they respectfully left. They were really very kind. What an awful job they had.

Once we were alone, Alex and I collapsed together on the sofa. We were both crying. There were no words. At one point he slammed his hand on the coffee table, but he was more composed than I was and trying to comfort me while his heart was breaking. Hysteria was hitting me in waves, and I needed help. I was the parent. I couldn't have my child taking care of me, and I had to get to my other child at Lawrenceville *right away*.

I reached for the phone, but my hand was shaking too

much to dial. "Call your uncle," I told Alex. Evan was there in fifteen minutes, my rock, taking charge. We couldn't let Chloe hear the news from anyone but us, and we needed her here with us. Evan reached her ice hockey coach, Nicole Uliasz, briefly filled her in, and added, "Please keep her with you, and obviously don't tell her anything. I'm on my way down to get her."

The instant he hung up Alex said, "I'm going with you."

If I'd been in my right mind, I would have been right behind them when they rushed out the door to bring Chloe home. Instead, in my shocked hysteria, all I could think was, "I can't let her see me like this." I asked them to tell her as little as possible beyond the headline that Rob had died so that I could be the one to break the awful details to her.

Chloe had wanted to come home that weekend. She'd texted Rob the night before and asked, "If I come home Saturday night could you drive me back to school on Sunday?" He'd texted back, "No, I'm sorry." She'd told him it was okay, and she was a little surprised when he'd replied, "I'm so sorry, Chloe." They'd had an especially good, close alone time together the previous Sunday when Rob drove her to and from her ice hockey game. They'd talked all the way there and all the way back about everything from their mutual love of history to what technology would be like in twenty years to school drama to you name it. And then there was the senior game we'd all gone to on Wednesday, when she'd presented him with his white Lawrence-ville hat. So what was up with the "I'm so sorry, Chloe"? It wasn't that big a deal.

For no reason she could imagine, she'd gone to sleep that Friday night feeling so sad she was almost in tears. She was still sad, down, as if there were some huge weight on her when she woke up the next morning and went to class. She's always been a happy, low-drama girl. She'd never felt like this before in her life, and she kept trying to shake it off as best she could. She didn't even mention it when, with her dad not available, she texted that morning to ask if I could bring her home and take her back to school the next day. We texted back and forth a few times. But then, inexplicably on her end, at around 10:00 A.M., I'd stopped answering her texts.

So when Alex and her uncle, Evan, showed up at her hockey coach's apartment, she was a little surprised; but she quickly jumped to the logical conclusion that they were there to pick her up because something had unexpectedly hijacked my day.

She went on high alert when, instead of greeting her with his usual brother-sister "Hey," Alex ordered her to sit down. She did, uneasily, with a predictable glare at him for bossing her around. Evan sat beside her and said, "I have some pretty bad news for you."

She had the same first thought Alex did—Grandpa's

dead—until he took a deep breath and added, "Chloe, there was an accident, and they couldn't save your dad."

She told me later that she suddenly felt completely separate from this whole scene, as if it were happening to someone else, and that somehow, irrationally and inexplicably, her mind leapt straight to, "Now who's going to walk me down the aisle?"

She started asking questions as Evan and Alex hurried her out of the apartment. They wouldn't answer her, just kept saying things like, "We don't know yet" and "We'll find out more when we get home." She spent the whole hour-and-a-half ride home piecing together stories in her head with not enough information and finally came up with a scenario that her father had been in a car accident, the doctors or paramedics screwed up somehow, and she'd lost her dad due to someone else's mistake.

When I finally took her into her bedroom and said, "Chloe, Dad killed himself. He jumped off the bridge," I realized what a horrible way it was for her to find out. To this day I regret not getting in that car with Evan and Alex and going to pick her up. I should have been the first one to walk into her hockey coach's apartment and tell her the news. All of it. It should all have come from me. It didn't. I shortchanged her at the most crushing moment she'd ever been through, and I'll always be sorry.

I had managed to make a few calls and send a few texts

after Evan and Alex left, and by the time they got home with Chloe the apartment was filling up.

My mom lived three floors below us in the same building. It alarmed her to see what terrible shape I was in when I answered the door. I told her about Rob, and she collapsed.

My best guy friend, Michael Asch, a successful New York City businessman whom I've known since the eighth grade, made it to my place in less than an hour.

My father was right behind him from his apartment in the city.

Then came my best girlfriend, Alice Kim, a doctor whose sister, also a doctor, had died by suicide six months earlier.

My practice administrator, Carole, my right hand for more than ten years, and Ana, my office nurse since 2004, had known and loved Rob and our kids for as long as they'd known and loved me. They heard the news and immediately began sobbing; but then, like the family they are to me, they took on the terrible task of making and taking a nonstop barrage of phone calls. They'd compose themselves, dial the next number, hear the person on the other end of the line break down when they explained the reason for the call, sensitively end the conversation with a few words of comfort and reassurance that Alex and Chloe and I were doing "as well as could be expected," hang up, fall apart again, recompose themselves, and move on to the next call. I'm sure it was agonizing for them, but they didn't hesitate to take it on, not for one minute.

Lisa Oz was there. Rob had been like a brother to her. She's one of the strongest women I've ever known, and she couldn't stop sobbing.

Barbara Fedida, ABC's Senior Vice President for Talent and Business and a close friend and colleague for eight years, sat with me and held my hand while I sobbed.

Flowers started arriving. People brought food. Word was spreading like wildfire, as were sorrow and utter disbelief. Someone had the good sense to close the blinds and cut us off from the looming, sickening view of the George Washington Bridge everywhere we turned.

There were tears and hugs and support all around me; but I was still in too much shock to take it in or even connect to it, as if I were watching the whole thing through the wrong end of a telescope.

Evan and Alex went across the street to Rob's apartment to feed and walk the Labs. While they were there Alex found the white Lawrenceville hat Chloe had bought Rob three nights before, still in its bag, the price tag still dangling from it, as if he knew what he was about to do and couldn't bring himself to wear it.

Alex also found three brief handwritten notes from Rob, one for each of us. Mine started, "First, no one is to blame." Chloe's ended with a catchphrase he'd been saying to her since she was five years old, something he said to her before every hockey game or texted her before games when he couldn't be there: "Skate hard and have fun."

She broke down when she read it.

THROUGH THIS HAZE OF CONVERSATIONS, CALLS, AND TEARS, only two moments managed to really penetrate the thick fog around me.

One was being alone in my bedroom with my brother. I finally said to him exactly what I was feeling, and what I imagined everyone else was thinking—"This is my fault." He put his hands on my shoulders, looked directly into my eyes, and said, "Jen, you're a doctor, I'm a doctor, Rob was a doctor. He would have done this married to you or not married to you. Divorce doesn't cause someone to commit suicide. The reality is, you cannot let this destroy you."

The other was being alone in my bathroom with Chloe, who suddenly cried out from the core of her soul, "Oh, my God, Mommy, please don't leave me."

To this day it's one of my most heartbreaking memories. I wrapped my arms around her and held her with every ounce of strength in me. "I'm not going to leave you," I promised her. "I'm not going anywhere."

Evan was right. I couldn't let this destroy me. I was the only parent my children had left. "You can't let this destroy you" became my mantra. My kids became my sole reason for putting one foot in front of the other, for not letting them see me fall completely apart and be afraid they were going to lose me too. Especially in those first twenty-four hours, and from that day forward, I was laser-focused on holding it together and taking care of them, rather than adding to the obscenely unfair nightmare they were going through by feeling as if they had to take care of me on top of it. Whatever it took, somehow or other, I was *not* going to let that happen.

Much easier said than done, but Alex and Chloe and I were in Dr. Simring's office the next day. Michael Asch had called within hours to tell her about Rob's suicide. She'd dealt with suicide survivors before. She'd even been one herself, in the sixth grade, when a cousin she was very close to shot himself in the head. Her family had handled it terribly. In fact, she knew nothing about it until she went to school the next day and a classmate shared a newspaper article about it during "Current Events." She'd learned, personally and professionally, that as hard as death and grieving are, suicide makes them even harder, because it's so stigmatized and is so often the result of clinical depression, i.e., a mental illness, which is also a stigma.

And of course Rob's death was particularly shocking to her. She hadn't seen him in about six months and didn't have a current sense of him; but she'd spent more than a year with him when he and I were trying to work on our marriage. She liked him, and she hadn't seen this coming at all. She'd immediately thought of what my kids and I would need and knew we'd need it urgently, no differently than if we'd had a heart attack and had to get to an emergency room ASAP; and she canceled her plans for that Sunday so she'd be available whenever we could get there.

Dr. Simring was a godsend. She told us a little about the "normal" responses to suicide—the blame, the guilt, the shock, the anger, the despair, the feeling rejected, the what-ifs—and explained that going through them all, and recognizing them as normal rather than questioning them and feeling guilty about them, is one of the first difficult steps toward healing. She gave me a few things to read, when and if I was ready, to help me begin to grasp the unimaginable why? of suicide. But mostly, she gave us a safe place to just express the overwhelming flood of intense, unfamiliar emotions we were drowning in, without judgment, without editing, without trying to apply logic to them or make sense of them.

It was exactly what we needed, when we couldn't have begun to know how much we needed it. I thought the session lasted about an hour. I found out later that it lasted more than three. I was still in shock, obviously, still feeling everything and nothing all at once and barely able to function, with virtually no sleep from the endless night before to keep me going.

People had kept arriving all that Saturday evening long. Some of Alex's closest friends showed up, including Tara, his best friend from high school, who flew in from St. Louis, where she was going to college, the minute she heard the news. Five of Chloe's closest friends drove three hours with their parents to be there and spend the night with her. Knowing my children were surrounded with lots of love and support, I finally disappeared into my bedroom and collapsed into bed. I've always been a good sleeper; but that night, lying there in the dark silence with my eyes closed, I discovered that my mind couldn't have cared less how exhausted my body was, it was too busy swirling around to let me rest.

Suicide. Rob died by suicide. I couldn't begin to wrap my head around it. That gentle man, deliberately doing something so violent, and terrifying, and isolated—what could possibly have pushed him to be so resolved to end his life that it overrode the most basic human instinct of survival? His love for our children was soul-deep. Endless. Incalculable. The pain that drove him over that bridge must have been massive to have overshadowed all that love, so massive that it couldn't reach him, couldn't make him stop and say, "I can't do this to them."

The divorce? Was that what caused him such massive pain? It couldn't be. He seemed fine with it. He seemed to not even care all that much. I was sitting right there, I heard him with my own ears tell Dr. Simring, when she asked us if we were having any thoughts of suicide, "No.

Absolutely not." Was he lying to her? Or had something happened to make him change his mind?

We'd never know, would we, because the only person who could tell us, and answer the countless other questions that were bound to come up, wasn't here anymore, would never be here again. How was that possible?

Was he at least at peace now? Was that how this worked? I hoped so.

Was it really that same morning that I'd been at Soul-Cycle, preoccupied with what my life was going to look like after our divorce, and how divorce was the worst thing that ever happened to me, and finding my way through feeling like a failure to regain my optimism? It seemed like a lifetime ago. I felt like a failure that morning? Really? Multiply it by about a million. . . .

"You can't let this destroy you."

"Oh, my God, Mommy, please don't leave me."

My children's father was gone. My children had lost their daddy. Suddenly I was the only parent they had. It made me unbearably sad, and unbearably frightened.

I'd never been one of those people who gave a lot of thought to death. I got it that it was inevitable, and I wasn't especially looking forward to it; but it wasn't something I thought about very often, certainly not anything I would have called an active fear. Now, out of nowhere, the fear of dying and leaving my children with no parent at all slammed into me. I couldn't let that happen. If it took becoming the most cautious person on this planet, if it took never riding in the back of a cab without my seat belt again, and certainly if it took giving up scuba diving— whatever it took, however much or little I had to say about it, Alex and Chloe would not become orphans. *Orphans?* Oh, God, whose mind had taken over and even let in that terrible word? Whose hell was I suddenly living?

Starting that night, and for weeks to come, I don't think I ever slept for more than two hours at a time. I couldn't sleep. I couldn't eat. I couldn't recognize myself, and the life I knew, in all this darkness. Maybe it was because, as of twelve short hours before, I wasn't whole anymore. Maybe it was because, twelve short hours before, I completely shattered.

CHAPTER TWO

B Y THE NEXT MORNING, THE SUICIDE OF DR. ROBERT ASHTON
was national news. Editors from *People* magazine, *News-week*, CNN, the local New York papers, you name it, were contacting ABC and/or my publicist, Heidi Krupp-Lisiten, wanting an interview with me, or at least a comment.

I don't think of myself as a celebrity or a public figure. But almost a decade on television comes with a spotlight whether you're aware of it or not, and the combination of a spotlight and the word *suicide* attracts the press like moths to a flame. The unavoidable headlines were, for the most part, salacious and suggestive, variations on the basic theme "Surgeon Jumps to His Death After Divorce from TV Personality Wife." In other words, "It's her fault, case closed, we hope she blames herself, because she deserves to." No problem there. I most certainly did blame myself, and it was excruciating.

ABC and Heidi were kind, vigilant, and very protective of me and my kids when it came to shielding us from the media. They thought it might satisfy at least some of the public curiosity if I posted an acknowledgment on social media ASAP; so with their help, and input from Alex and

Chloe, I found a beautiful, happy family photo of Rob, our kids, my parents, and me, along with the words "Our hearts are broken that the father of my teenage children took his own life yesterday."

At that point I didn't care anymore about legal technicalities than Rob did when he referred to me as his "wife" in the note he left for the police to find when they recovered his body. I wasn't about to refer to him as my "ex-husband." It seemed archaic, and dismissive of him, not to mention painfully irrelevant. He wasn't my ex-husband—he was Rob. My partner for the last twenty-one years of my life. My close friend. My coparenting teammate. Most of all, he was what he'll always be—my children's gentle, involved, adoring father. Besides, the focus belonged on Alex and Chloe, not on me. After a couple of rough drafts, I posted it as written.

I didn't stick around to read the comments. I'd been on social media long enough to know that some of them would be sincere and compassionate, while just as many if not more would be gleefully accusatory and downright vicious. My kids did read a lot of them and shielded me from many of them. I was grateful; but in the immediate aftermath of Rob's death, I can honestly say we were already at our saturation point when it came to pain, so the haters didn't even move the needle. And in the end, Alex and Chloe felt the same way I did about the countless people who make it their hobby to be anonymously cruel on the

Internet: Whoever you are, we're genuinely sorry your lives are so empty and unhappy that this is what you choose to put out there about yourselves. We won't engage, or get lured into a bunch of insipid debates, we'll just leave it at a simple, "Thanks for the information."

From that first day on, through days of disoriented mourning and three nights of shivah, we were never alone. At any given moment, there were anywhere from ten or fifteen to maybe a hundred people with us, along with enough food to feed a cruise ship for a week, literally dozens of flower arrangements, and an avalanche of sympathy cards. I knew those cards were well intended, but I couldn't bring myself to open a single one of them at that time—no matter how heartfelt the messages might have been, they seemed like one reminder after another after another that something unspeakably horrible had happened to my family.

My parents; my brother and sister-in-law and even some of their friends; Carole and Ana from my office; Dr. Mehmet and Lisa Oz and any number of other couples from Rob's and my inner circle; ABC friends and colleagues; dozens of my patients; Alex's schoolmates; Chloe's ice hockey teammates and coaches, even players and coaches from teams she'd played against over the years; not only my children's friends but their friends' parents as well—more people than I can begin to name or even remember were in and out of our apartment, many of them setting aside their own grief over Rob's death to offer whatever help we needed.

Incredibly, at one point I found myself in my living room with three other suicide survivors. There was my dearest friend Dr. Alice Kim, whose physician sister had killed herself just six months earlier; one of my patients, whose husband had taken his life a few years before; and another woman, also a physician, whose husband had shot himself in the past couple of years. It still amazes me. Twenty years earlier, to the best of my knowledge, I didn't know a single person who was struggling through a loved one's suicide. Now here sat four of us, together, in the same room. It was a tragic realization, and a comforting one. Almost without saying a word, those three women provided the same unique, invaluable support Dr. Simring had to offer. I didn't have to explain anything to them, or defend, or justify, or atone, or edit myself. They'd been where I was. They knew. And they'd survived it. I'd survive it too. I had to, for my children. I just couldn't imagine how.

Some of the greatest comfort came from unexpected places. One young man in particular really stood out. His name was Ormsby. He was a year ahead of Chloe at Lawrenceville, a boy she knew on sight but had never actually talked to. He texted her the night Rob died, introduced himself, and made the drive to our apartment to be with her the next day. He turned out to be a member of a student-run group called Friends Helping Friends, made up of students who'd been through the death of a parent. In his case, his father had died suddenly when Ormsby was younger; so while he hadn't experienced a parent's suicide, he'd been through a shocking tragedy that allowed him to understand Chloe's pain better than most. They're still great pals to this day, and she'll never forget his kindness toward a young stranger in despair. Neither will I. He's one of many who inspired her to say at the time, and continue to say a year and a half later, "I want to be *that* kind of friend."

Three of Rob's closest friends, going all the way back to their college years together, showed up bright and early on Wednesday morning. They were grieving too, of course, in deep pain; but they didn't let that interfere with the main reason they were there—they pulled Alex and Chloe aside and said, "Don't doubt for a second how much he loved you. You may have lost a dad, but you have three more of them right here." And they've stayed true to their word, with lots of texts and phone calls every single week without fail. It means the world to my kids, and it would have meant the world to Rob, that if they can't have their father, they can at least have his best friends.

Rob always remembered that, because of his medical specialty, his first question to the doctors when I was pregnant with Chloe and having my sonogram to check her anatomy was, "Is her heart good?" He knew that if her heart was good, she was good; and the heart became a special private symbol between the two of them. So a quiet moment with a hockey friend's mother, in the middle of all those people and all that surreal, dazed despair, took her breath away.

"I always have these in my pocket," her friend's mother said, "one for each of my kids. I've never told anyone I carry them, but something just came over me and I feel like you need one of them more than I do." She reached into her pocket, pulled something out, and put it in Chloe's hand. It was a little glass heart, about the size of a quarter. She'll always treasure it.

And then, sadly, maybe inevitably, there was that minority of mourners who became memorable for the wrong reasons, people you would have bet you could count on but turned out to exemplify the age-old observation that you really find out who your friends are—and who they're not—when a crisis hits.

A handful of people who insisted on "being there for us" turned out to be either trauma groupies who just wanted to be able to say they'd been there or gossips, hoping to dig up as much information as possible, since we were, after all, a national news story. They were so transparent they didn't even have the decency to be good at it. That wasn't helpful.

A couple of "friends" couldn't resist saying, "It must kill you to read the horrible things those Internet trolls are saying about you!" Gee, thanks for the reminder. That wasn't helpful.

One woman who had recently confided in me that she

desperately wanted to end her own marriage greeted me with a sympathetic hug, followed by, "When I told my husband what happened, he said, 'That's what men do when their wives divorce them. They kill themselves.'" That wasn't helpful.

A few colleagues of Rob's apparently thought it would be appropriate to tell me how furious they were with him for killing himself, spewing out words like *coward* and *selfish*. I was struggling with my own occasional spasms of anger, but my heart shifted straight into protective mode. Excuse me, I thought, but they were talking about a man they knew, a good man who'd apparently lost a tragically lonely battle with demons we couldn't begin to understand. These men were entitled to their feelings, they could just vent them to someone else. That wasn't helpful.

Then there was another of Rob's closest friends from college, a man I had grown to care about and love over the past two decades. He immediately stopped speaking to me the day Rob died and hasn't spoken to me since. So much for wondering who got his vote for "most likely person to blame," regardless of whether or not Rob would have agreed. Rather than be angry at him, my heart aches for him, but still, that wasn't helpful.

Through it all, I didn't hide, I just kept milling around that crowded apartment as if I were walking through wet cement. I took an antianxiety medication called Klonopin for a few days to try to put some distance between myself and my raw grief. All I really cared about was making sure I didn't fall apart and scare my children into thinking, "Oh, great, it's not bad enough we've lost our dad, now our mom is turning into a blubbering, incoherent wreck." I did manage not to cry in front of the mourners who were coming by to pay their respects. But at night, in the dark, after making sure Alex and Chloe were sound asleep in their rooms and surrounded by friends, I'd close my bedroom door, climb into bed, and quietly disintegrate.

On the third night I'd managed to slip into a restless sleep when I opened my eyes for an instant; and I swear to you, there was Rob, sitting on the edge of my bed right beside me, looking at me. His face was expressionless, but he seemed so serene—no sadness, no anger, no stress, no resentment, and certainly none of the injuries that would have been inevitable from the way he took his life. I remember his eyes, I remember the sense of peace around him, and I remember he had on a gray waffle-weave cotton shirt.

Needless to say, it startled me. A lot. In fact, I couldn't believe my eyes. I started crying, "No! No!" as I reached to put my hands on his shoulders. When I was almost touching him, he disappeared.

Nothing like that had ever happened to me before, and nothing like that has happened to me since. The temptation was to write it off as a dream, but the obvious question nagged at the back of my mind: what if it wasn't?

Then the autopsy report arrived. I couldn't bear to read it, so I had a doctor friend of mine take a look at it.

I asked if it mentioned what Rob was wearing when he killed himself.

It did. On the first page. Rob was wearing a gray cotton shirt.

That was all the confirmation I needed. I'm convinced, and I always will be, that it wasn't a dream. It wasn't some sleep-deprived grief hallucination. There's not a doubt in my mind that Rob's spirit paid me a visit that night. He might have come to say good-bye. He might have come to check on me. He might have come to show me that the death of his physical body didn't mean his spirit died with him—he was fine, he was perfectly intact, he was at peace, and he was around, keeping an eye on me and our children. Whatever the message, he was there. I know he was, and I feel blessed that I got to see him.

From what my doctor friend told me, by the way, the rest of the autopsy held no real surprises.

There were no drugs in Rob's system, and there was only a trace amount of alcohol.

His body was violently destroyed by his jump from the bridge. As a doctor, I'm graphically aware of the detailed impact on the human body of a two-hundred-foot fall. I'm still stuck with those images every time I close my eyes. But to compound the horror in Rob's case, he didn't land in the water, he landed on the rocks at the base of one of the steel stanchions that support the bridge. We'll never know for sure, of course, but our speculation is that he planned it that way. It's not unusual for bodies that end up in the Hudson River to go missing, sometimes forever. As unbearable as our reality was, it would have paled in comparison to the anguish of spending the rest of our lives wondering what happened to him, where he was, and whether or not he was dead or alive.

Obviously we didn't have to wonder. Rob was dead. That was an inescapable fact, and with that fact came the equally inescapable process of "making arrangements." I was running on fumes, barely functioning, which made me especially grateful that I already knew what Rob wanted and didn't want.

It was a tradition for us and a couple Rob and I were very close to throughout our marriage, with our five children in total, to spend every New Year's Eve together. Occasionally we'd lapse into conversations about death, funerals, cremation vs. burial, things like that—nothing depressing, really, just those talks among good friends about a subject we all think about but never discuss with anyone we don't know well. The four of us were so comfortable with each other that we could even get a little silly about it. The husband of the couple, for example, made it clear that not only did he want a funeral, but he also had his heart set on his wife and me being as dramatic at it as possible, shrieking, sobbing uncontrollably, and throwing ourselves on the casket.

Rob, on the other hand, was adamant every time the subject came up that he did *not* want a funeral. Period. He thought they were excruciating, maudlin, and a complete waste of money. He wanted his body to be either donated to a medical school or cremated, and for me to use whatever amount we would have spent on a funeral to take the kids on a trip to some place where our family had happy memories and celebrate his life rather than mourn his death.

Those conversations never seemed depressing when we were having them. I guess I never connected them to reality, or let it sink in that I might actually outlive him. At eighteen and no longer a minor, Alex was Rob's legal next of kin, and we made arrangements based on what Rob had emphatically said he wanted. Donating Rob's body to a medical school wasn't an option, for obvious reasons. That left Plan B. My practice administrator and Rock of Gibraltar, Carole, went with me to the funeral home to make cremation arrangements. I could never have done it by myself or put my children through taking me. Carole didn't say, "Would you like me to go with you?" She said, "I will take you." The difference is huge at times like that.

We honored the last of Rob's wishes in March, when Alex, Chloe, my parents, and I spent six peaceful, healing days in Jamaica. Our family had enjoyed many vacations there, and we loved it so much that we'd had Chloe's bat mitzvah in Jamaica a few years earlier. (We jokingly called it her rasta mitzvah.) The trip in March was the first time we'd all been away together, separate from the inevitable commitments, distractions, and noise of our daily lives, and the constant visual reminders of what happened. For the first time since February 11, I could focus all my energy on my children and just "being"; and every once in a while I actually felt tiny glimmers of my health and energy starting to come back.

On one of those six mornings I looked out my hotel room window and saw a full, perfect rainbow arced over the sea. It might have just been a rainbow. Or it might have been a thank-you from Rob, for bringing our kids to a place where our family had been happy together once upon a time.

I know which I prefer to believe, and thank you for suggesting it in the first place, Rob. We know it's exactly what you would have wanted.

SHORTLY BEFORE OUR TRIP TO JAMAICA, MY KIDS CAME UP WITH an idea that was just what we all needed. I wish it had been my idea, but when they first broached the subject I was in no shape to think of anything other than putting one foot in front of the other and remembering to breathe.

It was the second night of shivah. Every square inch of our apartment was filled with people and flowers and food, and I escaped into my bedroom for a few minutes to regroup and reinforce my determination to remain vertical. Alex and Chloe followed me inside and closed the door. They obviously had something on their minds; and I prayed that whatever it was, whatever they needed, I could summon the strength and the clarity to do it and do it right.

So when Alex announced, "Mom, Chloe and I have talked it over, and we can't continue to live in this apartment," it was a huge relief. I wanted so desperately to do something to help them through this, something more than loving them, holding them, listening to them, making sure they weren't alone if they didn't want to be, spending time with Dr. Simring, anything and everything I could think of. But moving out of our apartment, an apartment full of memories that had turned brutally painful? Something tangible and active and "busy" to distract me from our relentless, excruciating grief? Something I knew how to do, and do well, that would make a real difference to them? Not just yes, but yes, *please*!

"I can have us out of here in forty-eight hours," I told them. "I'll walk out of here right now and never set foot in this apartment again if that's what you need."

They assured me it wasn't quite that urgent—it was only February, after all, and they'd be going back to school. If we could find a new place for them to come home to by the time summer rolled around, that would be great.

A few good friends, worth their weight in gold and then some, had already suggested that getting out of that apartment, away from Rob's apartment right across the street, and out from under the shadow of the George Washington Bridge would be a wise, healthy thing to do. Lisa and Mehmet Oz had invited us to move in with them, as soon as we wanted for as long as we wanted; and Michael Asch had told me, "You've got to get your kids out of here and find a place in the city that will give the three of you a fresh start."

(I still smile when I look back on that conversation. As I mentioned, Michael's a very successful businessman, and he lives in a spectacular penthouse. His recommendation that I find an apartment in the city came with the added brainstorm that I rent a place "with lots of outdoor space to really enhance the New York experience." He said it matter-of-factly, with a straight face. It was so Michael. If he does something, he *does* it. Big. I remember laughing a little at that advice. It was like needing a car and having a friend say, "You should get a Bentley. They're reliable, and really comfortable, and you can't beat the trunk space." Nice idea, and God knows he meant well, but there's this thing called reality. . . .)

Finding a new home for my kids and me went straight to the top of my priority list; and on Wednesday, February 15, Alex, Chloe, and I headed into the city to meet a smart, warm, fantastic realtor named Richie Herschenfeld, an appointment arranged by Barbara Fedida, to look at apartments. When I'd told Barbara that I needed to get my kids out of that apartment, she had launched into action by connecting me with Richie, with the promise that, "He'll take care of you. He's amazing."

To make the trip to our appointment with Richie that morning presented a challenge I'd been silently dreading—the quickest way to get there was to cross the George Washington Bridge.

When we got to our car Alex gently took the keys from me and said, "Mom, you haven't been over the bridge yet. Why don't I drive?" My strong, sensitive son was trying to take care of me. Both my children had been trying to take care of me for days, the exact opposite of how this was supposed to go as far as I was concerned. I was in awe of their courage and sensitivity. It took me a long time to figure out that they needed to help their mom every bit as much as I needed to help them. But when it came to crossing the bridge, I relented, just this once and let Alex drive.

We all looked over at that horrible spot as we drove past it, the spot where Rob had very deliberately stopped walking, climbed up on the railing, and jumped to his death. It was impossible not to picture it. It was frightening and literally sickening to imagine those last few seconds, and the black hole of despair that led up to them and propelled him there. Was he afraid at the end, or crying? Or was he calm and resigned, not feeling anything at all? What happened to push him over the edge? Or what hadn't happened? And how were our kids and I ever supposed to make peace with the fact that we'd never know why?

There's still a deep ache when I drive across the George Washington Bridge, but it passes more quickly than it used to. I've stopped expecting it to go away completely.

Richie Herschenfeld made it worth the trip. Barbara Fedida had filled him in on our situation so that we didn't have to; and he took incredible care of us, treating us with kid gloves and compassion as he showed us some great affordable apartments he'd already arranged for us to see. That night Alex found one on the Internet that looked comfortable, convenient on the west side of Manhattan, and exactly right.

Yet another friend went far out of her way—about six hours out of her way, in fact—to look at that apartment with Alex and me. Shelley Looney, Olympic gold and silver ice hockey medalist and one of my closest friends, drove all the way from Buffalo, New York, to be there in the city with us. She'd lived with our family several years earlier for about six months, knew all of us including Rob very well, of course, and she wanted to help by being part of the apartment-hunting process. So on Thursday Richie showed Alex, Shelley, and me the apartment Alex had found, and I signed the lease on Friday. Moving day was May 1, a little more than two months later, far enough away to be feasible and soon enough to give my kids what they needed, which made it what I needed too.

Chloe headed back to Lawrenceville that same Thursday, February 16. Alex went back to Columbia a couple of days later. Alex had exams coming up, and Chloe felt as if she had to get away from all that oppressive sadness and all those reminders of the happiest and the most devastating times of her life if she was ever going to get better.

The support that was waiting for her at school was jaw-dropping. Her coach, Nicole Uliasz, had already talked to her headmaster, her teachers, and her teammates; and they were all eager to make things as easy as possible for her. "Come back to class when you're ready," she was told. "Come back to hockey practice when you're feeling up to it." "You don't have to take final exams." "Don't worry about homework." Everything she could possibly have needed, Nicole had anticipated it and seen to it, including offering that Chloe sleep at her apartment for the first couple of nights so she wouldn't be alone.

With a few exceptions, her friends, like mine, rallied around her. It's impossible to put into words how much those friends mean when you're at a point in your life that's lower than anything you ever imagined. You never forget those friends, and there's nothing you wouldn't do for them to reciprocate.

Her few exceptions, like mine, were just as unforgettable.

If nothing else, they teach you what *not* to do when there's someone in your life who has their back to the wall. A handful of her classmates suddenly wanted nothing to do with her and almost went out of their way to avoid her. It's entirely possible that they distanced themselves simply because they had no idea how to approach someone who's in the unique despair of grieving a suicide; but it felt to her as if they were angry with her, or maybe resenting her for the support and attention she was getting, support and attention she would have traded in a heartbeat for a chance to have her father back. A genuine "I'm so sorry" is all it would have taken, and it would have made such a difference.

The "what *not* to do" award from Chloe's first days back at Lawrenceville goes to the "friend" who, in response to the compassionate lenience extended to her by the faculty and coaches, said behind her back, "Chloe seems to expect a free pass around here because her dad died." When it got back to her, she didn't dignify it with a response, she simply made a mental note to never, ever say such a thing to or about anyone, and, as best she could, to learn to expect being occasionally blindsided like that and quietly distance herself from those people who obviously weren't who she thought they were. In other words, again, thanks for the information.

Despite her coach Nicole's invitation to take her time coming back to practice, Chloe was on the ice with her teammates that first day; and Evan, his wife and kids, and

I went to her game a couple of nights later. My father was there too. Evan and I wore Chloe's team jerseys as a show of support, something we'd never done before.

It was brutally hard for all of us. Rob was the quintessential hockey dad, at nearly every one of Chloe's games since she was five years old. Evan and I couldn't imagine how she was able to even get on the ice that night, knowing he wasn't there and knowing why. I could tell that, understandably, she was unfocused and all over the place. When she got a penalty at the end of the first period, which was unusual for her, I knew things were coming apart. Nicole knew it too, and she gave her the options of getting back on the ice, sitting on the bench, or changing clothes and calling it a night. Chloe made her choice clear when she skated off to the locker room, and I followed her.

I found my daughter alone in the locker room, angry, crying, and emotionally out of control. I was moving toward her to hold her when she clenched her fists and cried out, "Why wasn't I enough?!"

It crushed my heart. We knew from Dr. Simring that feeling self-blame and rejection is among the unavoidable responses to suicide, and that it's part of the healing process to go through those responses rather than hide from them. But knowing it intellectually and accepting it emotionally are two entirely different things. It was unbearable that, even for a second, Chloe thought she had anything to do with her father killing himself, and that the only person who could possibly convince her of that wasn't there anymore. I immediately thought to myself, "Oh, my God, I'm not going to be enough of a mom to be Mom *and* Dad for my sweet children. I can't fix this."

At the same time, I couldn't deny that I knew exactly how she felt. For the last ten years of our marriage, I'd sensed Rob withdrawing from me. I didn't understand why, or what to do about it, but I came to the conclusion that somehow it was my fault, my inadequacy, my failure. As our relationship devolved I became convinced that he didn't want to be married to me anymore, which meant I didn't want to be married to him anymore either. He used to say, "All I need to be happy are my books and my dogs." Okay. Got it. Enough said.

No doubt about it, our divorce was amicable. Nobody left anybody. But privately, deep down inside, I felt he'd left me ten years earlier. The thought just hadn't fully crystallized, and I don't think I'd fully mourned the slow disintegration of our marriage, and our divorce, until he took his life and *really* left me. He was never coming over to our apartment again. He wasn't living right across the street anymore. He was gone.

Why wasn't *I* enough?

And when he withdrew from me all those years ago— had he really withdrawn from life in general, and I just hadn't noticed?

The questions were endless. I trusted Dr. Simring

enough to be sure that I had to let myself ask them, and feel them, in order to start the slow process of healing; but my God, they hurt like hell.

Dr. Simring also warned us that, for quite some time, it would be normal not to feel normal. She couldn't have been more right.

Alex, who's always made friends and fit in among his peers with the greatest of ease, was feeling "different" and "separate" because he knew he was the guy whose father had jumped off the George Washington Bridge.

Chloe, who'd always loved school and loved hockey, often found herself thinking of them as stupid, meaningless, as if they couldn't possibly matter less. It was so jarring to her that she'd stare into the mirror and not even recognize the girl staring back at her, although she didn't look any different.

And I could barely bring myself to glance at mirrors and confront the fact that I looked horrible. I'd lost nine pounds in eleven days, and I didn't have a spare nine pounds to lose. My inability to sleep more than an hour or two at a time had taken its toll on my eyes, which were now dark and sunken. The tension of chronic pain shows in the face; and I was literally in such physical pain from grieving that it surprised me to not find bruises.

Maybe most jarring and not normal of all, though, was how little I cared. All my life I'd taken great pride and pleasure in how I looked. It was part of my general "striving for perfection" thing. I loved makeup. I loved clothes, and fashion, and the whole toilette process of getting ready to go out or go on the air. Now I was avoiding mirrors for days at a time, partly because of this sudden apathy about pulling myself together and partly because I'd become such a shadow of myself that I thought I might be disappearing. Or maybe disappearing was exactly what I wanted to do.

I'm a doctor. I've studied the physical effects of grief on the human body. I was a walking illustration of those effects; and I wasn't doing a thing about it, when I of all people should have known better. If I didn't turn this around, I'd end up in the hospital. Just what my children needed, their mom, the only parent they had left, lying in a hospital bed, wasting away.

Slowly but surely, I started forcing myself to eat something every few hours, and I recruited my friend and trainer Cliff to meet me at the gym in our building and ease me back into working out. Exercising was the only time I didn't feel numb. It helped enormously, even though it didn't seem like it at the time. As for sleep, that would have to come naturally—I'd given up on Klonopin after a few days, and I'd tried Ambien for a week, which didn't help either. But maybe putting some effort into taking care of myself again, and getting some exercise, would at least make a little difference.

It wasn't as if I had a choice, and not just for my kids.

Ready or not, I had to go back to work.

CHAPTER THREE

C AROLE AND ANA HAD BEEN DOING A FANTASTIC JOB OF HOLD-
ing down the fort at my office, rescheduling patients,
referring them to generous colleagues who'd offered to do
anything they could to help, just making sure in general
that my patients were well taken care of and that I'd still
have a practice to go back to when I was ready.

Taking a few months off might have been understandable, but emotionally and financially it wasn't an option.
Dr. Simring and I had talked many times about the fact
that the element of routine is vastly important to people
who are dealing with profound shock and grief, to remind
them that their whole lives haven't been blown apart. Alex
and Chloe were back in school, back to their routines, so
I couldn't expect more of them than I expected of myself.

I'm also not a celebrity millionaire who only works
when my yacht's in dry dock for repairs. (For the record,
I don't happen to own a yacht.) I love my work, but I also
depend on it, and so do my kids. In fact, I'd been the primary breadwinner in our household since Rob changed
careers in 2012. Now it was just me, and I had bills to pay.
I had a staff relying on me for their salaries. I had a son in

college and a daughter in boarding school. Two weeks to be "ready" to head back to my office was literally all I could afford.

As for my TV career, everyone at ABC, from ABC Television President Ben Sherwood and President of ABC News James Goldston on down, had been kind, compassionate, and understanding beyond belief. They'd told me to take as much time as I needed before coming back to *Good Morning America*. I'd arbitrarily told them six weeks should be enough.

What I didn't tell them, because I was struggling with it a lot, was that I wasn't one bit sure I'd ever be able to face going back on the air at all.

The fact that I looked terrible was only part of it. There was a whole other issue to deal with that I hated, and that I kept telling myself shouldn't matter. But as we all know, there's often a big difference between how things should be and how they are.

It was described perfectly by one of my three suicide-survivor girlfriends who'd been with me one night at shivah, the one whose husband had shot himself a couple of years earlier. "I have to tell you," she said, "everywhere I go I feel as if people look at me differently. It's like I have a scarlet letter on my chest."

Exactly. A scarlet letter on her chest, and she wasn't a public figure. Her husband's suicide hadn't been national news. I'd already experienced the feeling that some people were looking at me differently. I didn't know how or if I could handle the feeling of literally millions of people seeing that scarlet letter on my chest, speculating on what profound character failure either had caused me to miss the signs that Rob was suicidal or had actually propelled him over the railing of a bridge. So much for that image of perfection and success I'd cultivated all my life. I was obviously flawed, badly. I couldn't imagine parading that fact on *Good Morning America* for the world to see.

Fortunately, I didn't have to make that decision right away. My staff and my patients needed my immediate attention; and, as I quickly discovered, I needed theirs too.

Carole and Ana had arranged a half schedule for me so that I could ease my way back into my routine. They also knew me well enough to know that I was struggling to concentrate in general, and that I was drowning in a double dose of legal and logistical issues, both from Rob's death and from some residual post-divorce technicalities as well. What little was left of me walked into my office that first day just praying I could stay focused. Going back to work wasn't only about paying my bills, or getting back to a routine. It was literally about life-and-death issues for my patients. It required concentration. I took a deep breath as I tackled the pile of lab results, mammogram reports, sonogram reports, and other medical tests that were waiting for me on my desk. As far as I was concerned, the fact that I was there meant I was fully prepared to give my patients the care they'd come to expect from me after our many years together.

What I wasn't expecting was the care I got from them. Hundreds of sympathy cards were waiting in bins beside my desk. Every single patient greeted me with hugs, and cried with me, and, before I had a chance to ask questions about them, asked about me instead—how was I doing, what did I need, and how could they help? Patient after patient, day after day, extended nothing but kindness. They didn't just make me feel accepted and unjudged, they inspired me to think more times than I can count, as Chloe put it, "I want to be *that* kind of friend."

There was one patient in particular I want to acknowledge on paper, as an example of how far out of their way some people will go to help someone in distress, and as a reminder to all of us, including me, that sometimes, by just paying attention and being creative, we can anticipate a way to help and take care of it without waiting to be asked.

Alex and Chloe had brought Rob's two Labrador retrievers, Nigel and Remy, home to our apartment a few days after Rob took his life. Until then, they'd taken turns going across the street to Rob's to walk them and feed them, and probably just to spend time at their dad's place. Technically Nigel and Remy were our family's dogs, along with our Morkie, Mason, and we adored them; but from the moment Rob laid eyes on them when they were puppies, Nigel and Remy were his, and he was theirs, their "alpha dog," their best friend, and their favorite playmate.

By now they were elderly for Labs, twelve or thirteen years old, high maintenance and grieving the loss of the two-legged leader of their pack. One of Rob's dearest friends and the best man at our wedding, who also happens to be a great dog lover, knew how close Nigel and Remy were to Rob. He also knew that they might be more of a handful than I could manage by myself under the circumstances. He was right. So, without being asked, he offered to give them a wonderful home with him and his family if that would be helpful. Alex and Chloe and I agreed that Nigel and Remy would be adored and beautifully cared for by Art and said yes and thank you eight or nine hundred times.

There was just one problem: Nigel and Remy were with us in New Jersey. Art lived in Florida.

Next thing I knew, my patient Staci, who'd heard the story and was also a dog lover, took it upon herself to arrange for a private car company that transports pets to deliver our sweet Labs to their new home a thousand miles away, where they're living happily ever after. When I literally felt I couldn't trust myself to get through a day, Staci found a service I could trust with Rob's dogs' lives, to take them kindly and safely to Florida.

With everything that was going on, I could never have

made those arrangements. And I would never have asked Staci or anyone else for such a huge, complicated favor.

I have no idea how I ever can repay her, and Art, and too many other people to name. I just hope that if and when someone in distress in my life needs a similar favor they haven't even thought of yet, I can be as thoughtful, and as gifted at anticipating it and taking care of it, as Staci was for me.

And while I was still shattered, the compassion of my patients, my staff, and Dr. Simring was helping a piece or two of me fall back into place—very small pieces, but it was a start.

I couldn't give my children the message that their mom's answer to tragedy was to hide while they were being so strong and getting back in the game.

I couldn't let my pride jeopardize my family's financial security.

I couldn't dismiss my long-standing commitment to people who'd been nothing but kind, loyal, and protective of me.

Dr. Simring had pointed out more than once that "a nonsuicidal person, when things are at their darkest and their worst, says, 'Tomorrow will be better. This can't go on forever.' They can see their way out of it. The suicidal person, when things are at their most dismal, says, 'Tomorrow will be worse, and I have to get out of this now.'" It made me unbearably sad to think of Rob feeling that way, even for a second. It also motivated me. In my heart of hearts, I really did believe that tomorrow could be better, and it was up to me to try to make it happen.

I picked up the phone, called ABC, and told them I was ready to come back.

On March 22, just under six weeks since Rob's suicide, I walked into the *Good Morning America* studios. If people thought I looked haggard and imperfect, oh, well. I did, and I was. If they couldn't get past that scarlet letter on my chest, oh, well. I wasn't there to be "that woman whose husband killed himself." I was there to be Dr. Jennifer Ashton, at that time Senior Medical Contributor, and soon to be Chief Medical Correspondent, for the network and for *GMA*, to discuss the cancer risk of breast implants. And if I got emotional and broke down during my segment, oh, well. I'd try my best not to, but there's only so much you can control on live TV.

I'd been bolstered and very touched by an e-mail from Ben Sherwood the night before. It read, "Greetings from Buenos Aires—sorry to miss your return tomorrow morning—but just wanted to wish you the very best. Sending a big hug. And strength. We've missed you. So glad you're back." The president of ABC Television taking the time to send me such a warm, thoughtful note from halfway around the world made such a difference. He cared, it mattered to him that I was showing up the next day, and I didn't want to disappoint him and my other ABC bosses.

A lot of large companies love to claim that they're a "family," whether or not they even know their employees' first names. If I'd ever doubted that ABC News and *Good Morning America* really were and are my "work family," those doubts were erased the minute I stepped through the studio door that morning. Hundreds of people are involved in putting *GMA* on the air, and I'm not exaggerating when I say that every one of them I came in contact with, from the security guards, to the cameramen, to the stage managers, to the audio crew and lighting technicians, to my hair and makeup team and wardrobe stylists, greeted me with nothing but the pure, nonjudgmental love and support of a family. They could feel how hard it was for me; and their hugs, eye contact, and kind words made it clear that they were right there with me, they had my back, and not for one moment was I alone. A couple of them even confided in me that they knew what I was going through because they'd lost a loved one to suicide, they'd just never said anything because they didn't think anyone would understand and they didn't want to make their coworkers uncomfortable. I felt privileged to be able to give them the same hugs they'd just given me. We're even closer now than we were before.

Barbara Fedida never left me from the moment I stepped through the door. I spent time with Robin Roberts in her dressing room before we went on the air together, and I said yes to her asking if she could say a few personal words to me at the end of our segment. She and I go back more than five years. I trust her, I admire her, and I respect her more than I have words to describe. There's no one I would rather have had by my side that day. I'd watched in awe as she publicly battled her own life-threatening health issues and wondered at the time where she got the strength. Now I was wondering where I'd find the energy and the fire to lift myself out of my own despair; but there sat Robin, my inspiration for on-air courage and grace under duress, and her presence bolstered me.

Cameras rolled. Robin and I talked about the possible link between silicone breast implants and a rare blood cancer. I could peripherally see Barbara Fedida and ABC's Vice President of Talent and Development Mary Noonan standing nearby like my emotional bodyguards, and *GMA* anchors Amy Robach and George Stephanopoulos just a few feet away, on set, with silent, empathetic "You got this!" smiles. I knew that inside the control room there were dozens of producers and directors at the ready to take the camera shot off of me if I decompensated. I felt their love and support like a safety net beneath me.

Then, as the segment ended, Robin said, on the air, "You know, Jen, we're so glad that you're back, and our thoughts are with you and your children."

At that moment I knew that, thanks to all these amazing people around me, and nine years of on-camera muscle memory, I was going to be okay. Choking back my tears, I realized I could do this. I was still in a fog, still struggling to focus, but even if it was only subconsciously at the time, I was learning a lot.

Yes, getting back to a familiar routine was very helpful. Many months later, I met a woman whose husband had killed himself not long after Rob did, by jumping out their apartment window. She didn't work outside the home, and her pain and grief were still as raw as they were the day it happened. I was lucky to have a routine to go back to, surrounded by people who cared. I was even lucky that financially I had no choice. If it hadn't been a necessity, if money hadn't been an issue, I'm not sure I would have made myself return to work; and without that reminder that there was life after Rob, life after suicide, I can't imagine how long I might have been emotionally frozen in a dark, awful place.

Yes, most people really want to help in a terrible crisis; and they can, and do, possibly more than they'll ever know, with the simplest gestures of kindness. I didn't think of this part until much, much later, but maybe, without realizing it, I was able to reciprocate a little. It was undoubtedly helpful to my staff, my patients, my ABC colleagues, and my friends to see me back at work—not because of me, but because it's always reassuring to see anyone who's been through a nightmare wake up from it and keep going, no matter how slowly. Who doesn't need the message from time to time, spoken or unspoken, "You can get through this"?

Dr. Simring had given me some reading material on that first day for when and if I was able to concentrate enough to read at all. I still wasn't able to absorb more than a few sentences at a time, but I did come across a thought or two that made sense to me and brought me some comfort.

One was from a book called *The Noonday Demons*, by Andrew Solomon. The last paragraph of the chapter on suicide begins, "I would say of suicide not that it is always a tragedy for the person who died but that it always comes too soon and too suddenly for those left behind."

She also gave me a brilliant, very insightful article from the May 23, 2013, issue of *Newsweek*, called "Why Suicide Has Become an Epidemic—And What We Can Do to Help," by Tony Dokoupil. I read the last paragraph over and over again:

"It's not easy to get people into treatment. There's the cost, for one thing, but more than that, there's the shame and the stigma. Suicide is the rare killer that fails to inspire celebrity PSAs, 5K fun runs, and shiny new university centers for study and treatment. That has to change. . . . We need to get it in our heads that suicide is not easy, painless, cowardly, selfish, vengeful, self-masterful, or rash. . . . And once we get all that in our heads at last, we need to let it lead our hearts."

I remember being inspired by that, and not having a clue what to do about it.

In the meantime, my great friends were seeing to it that I didn't fall into the potentially self-destructive habit of just coming home from work and holing up in my apartment day after day, night after night. They'd take me out to dinner a few nights a week, and we'd talk about pretty much anything but grieving. And every once in a while, to my quiet alarm, I'd find myself laughing, or feeling normal again for a moment or two, or simply enjoying myself, immediately followed by the most awful guilt. It had only been weeks since Rob had taken his life, since my children's father had killed himself. The kids were struggling to recover from the most devastating loss of their young lives; everyone who knew him, including me, had lost a man they loved and admired; and here I was occasionally having a good time as if everything was fine? How could I? Shame on me!

Which led to another valuable lesson during that terrible, confusing time, again thanks to Dr. Simring. In what almost amounted to a confession, I told her about this inappropriate side of myself that had started revealing itself.

"What the hell is wrong with me?" I asked her, in tears.

"Nothing," she said. "What you're going through is a normal part of healing—it's not just normal, it's healthy. It's called 'multiple truths.'"

"Multiple truths" means that you can feel opposite ends of the emotional spectrum at the same time without one of those feelings negating the validity of the other. You can be in the worst, most gut-wrenching grief and still laugh, or feel something positive, or even fall in love, and it doesn't diminish the depth and sincerity of your grief. As Dr. Simring emphasized, it's not choosing grief *or* laughter, it's accepting and not judging the fact that grief *and* laughter can and do coexist—"multiple truths," both of them real and perfectly appropriate; so essentially, don't beat yourself up about them, embrace them as a sign that you're making progress.

It was a breakthrough for me, and a big relief. I realized I'd been trying to push away any feelings of happiness and hopefulness, thinking they were disrespectful to Rob's memory. But would Rob really have wanted to leave our children and me a legacy of misery for the rest of our lives? Of course not. That's not who he was. And ready or not, looking forward was an inescapable part of my reality, with moving day, May 1, getting closer and closer.

I've always loved moving. I know to some people that's like saying I've always loved root canals. But it's like a new beginning to me, a new phase, a clean slate; and I also love the whole nesting and organizing facets of turning a blank, empty space into a warm, comfortable, welcoming home.

There was no question that our move from Fort Lee into an apartment in New York City was emotionally essential for my kids, and in some ways for me as well. I was excited about it because they were excited about it. I appreciated the busyness of it, and the chance to tackle a big challenge I

happen to be good at. And all of us were beyond ready to escape our relentless view of the George Washington Bridge.

For the first time in my life, packing and moving
brought a bittersweet sense of heaviness with them. Rob
had already moved out of that apartment and into his own
place many months earlier, when we first separated. But
he'd also lived in that apartment for a year, back when we
were still married and trying to make things work; and
as I stared at stacks of boxes, I was surprised to feel such
a tangible connection to him, a connection I hadn't felt
during our divorce. I'd reach to open the refrigerator door,
for example, and find myself thinking, "Rob touched this
handle," or glance over at the bathroom sink and be almost
amazed that once upon a time, Rob stood there shaving.
It felt like even more of a good-bye that our new apartment on the west side would be the first place I'd lived
in twenty-two years that Rob would never come walking
into, or even see. The finality stopped me in my tracks
more than once as I tried to wrap my head around the idea
that "never" really did mean *never*.

Now, roll your eyes if you want, but I don't move into
a new home or office without booking an appointment
with a man I met several years ago who happens to be an
international feng shui consultant. (He also happens to
be Swiss. Go figure.) He's wonderful at helping arrange
furniture and belongings in a way that promotes the most
beneficial energy flow, and at cleansing and blessing a new

space. Feng shui is either truly beneficial or it's truly beneficial because I *believe* it's truly beneficial. Either way, I don't
see a downside to hedging my bets, and I really value this
man and his input.

He'd met Rob when we moved to Fort Lee, and he
liked him; so it was natural for the subject of Rob's death
to come up when he met me at the new apartment for our
consultation. "You know," he said, "in case you're not already aware of this, there are some cultures that don't think
of suicide as a dark, evil act at all. They believe that people
making the choice of when and how they die is a beautiful,
sacred life ritual."

I had no idea, and told him so.

He quickly added, "I'm not trying to suggest that suicide is a good thing. I just want you to have the global and
cultural perspective that the stigma our culture attaches to
it isn't embraced around the world."

I tried to imagine a culture in which Alex and Chloe
and I could miss Rob and grieve for him without the added
pain of guilt, blame, and shame. I couldn't.

He sat down beside me. "Jen, I've worked with several
people whose families have been affected by suicide, and
so many of them have told me they feel they don't have
'closure.' I've thought about you and Rob a lot since the
day he took his life. Please know that I made contact with
his spirit, and he made a clean break. Rob's at peace."

I flashed back to that night in February when I opened

my eyes to find Rob sitting beside me on my bed in his gray shirt, looking at me. My friend was right. Rob was at peace. His pain was gone. His despair was over. I needed to keep remembering that. I needed to keep hoping that maybe one good thing had come out of this after all.

The new apartment was unpacked, organized, feng shui'd, and ready by the time Alex and Chloe got back from school. They loved it the instant they walked through the door, and I loved knowing I'd given my kids a home they'd look forward to instead of dreading. I'd made sure to keep their father's presence alive in our new home, with lots of happy photos of him with them, him with his best friends, and him with all of us on display. I'd put a lot of those photos away when Rob and I were going through our divorce—amicable or not, I don't know too many people who enjoy looking at pictures of their soon-to-be-ex spouses everywhere they turn. But that seemed like ancient history now. He belonged here, smiling at us. I even put special effort into decorating the kitchen in his honor. Rob was a brilliant cook, and *brilliant* is not too strong a word. I, on the other hand, have to Google instructions on how to boil water. Rob would have appreciated a nice kitchen, so I made sure that our kids and I would have one whether I ever used it or not.

In fact, I put another finishing touch on the kitchen a few days ago, while writing this book. Rob and I had taken a wonderful trip to Florence, Italy, in 2006, for our tenth wedding anniversary. We were browsing one day in this lovely antique art store and came across the most charming little two-by-two-inch two-hundred-year-old paintings, one for each letter of the alphabet. We bought our initials, "R" and "J," and also "A" and "C," for Alex and Chloe. I wasn't sure what I was going to do with the "R" during our separation. Giving that one to Rob seemed weird, so I just kept all four; and now all four letters are on our kitchen wall, artistically (more or less) arranged around the light switches. Dr. Simring promised us over and over again that, with enough time and enough healthy healing, the day would come when our memories of Rob would make us smile rather than cause us pain. A year and a half later, those little antique initials in the kitchen make me smile.

Alex and Chloe finished their school years with a lot of hard work in their classes and on themselves, keeping up sessions on the phone with Dr. Simring and letting themselves experience whatever they were feeling without judgment or editing.

Alex, for the most part, was just sad, and processed his father's suicide with great compassion. "Dad had a disease, like cancer, and it killed him. I wouldn't be angry with someone who died of cancer, so how can I be angry with him?" He was grateful to have his college courses to focus on and was headed off that summer for a month to study economics and finance at the London School of Economics. I was very aware, whether he was or not, that in the several weeks since Rob's death, he was strongly, gently becoming the man of the family, watching out for his sister and me without making an issue of it; and every time I thought I couldn't possibly love and admire him more, he proved me wrong.

Chloe was making progress with her feelings and her anger, not judging them, just recognizing how easy it would be to walk around with a big chip on her shoulder and refusing to let that happen. A very upset classmate came flouncing up to her one night, for example, and announced, "I just had the worst day *ever*! My boyfriend broke up with me!" Chloe resisted the impulse to reply, "Really? That's your worst day ever? On my worst day ever my father jumped off a bridge and killed himself." She caught herself several times, in situations like that, almost resenting people who hadn't been through a real tragedy. But then she'd force herself to acknowledge that not too long ago, she'd never been through a real tragedy either, and whatever problems she was having back then felt like a big deal to her.

She was also doing her best to take Dr. Simring's advice about struggling to recognize herself: "Remember who you were and what your goals were before your father's suicide. Then just try to be patient and honor that 'you' while you work on feeling normal again. You worked too hard on your grades and hockey to let this one tragedy throw it all away." She'd find herself going through the motions a lot;

but from time to time she'd get occasional twinges of her old enthusiasm, and they kept her going.

A colleague of Rob's, a Boston businessman named Mark Adams, had called shortly after Rob's suicide to offer his condolences and ask if there was anything he could do to help. He particularly remembered how Rob loved to brag about what an incredible ice hockey player Chloe is—a subject close to Mark's heart, since his own sons play at the elite level, and his youngest son was even drafted by the NHL.

"You know," he said, "if Chloe intends to play ice hockey in college, she needs to train with Paul Vincent. He's holding a hockey camp in Cape Cod this summer, and I'd be happy to make that connection for her if you think she'd be interested."

She was, and thanks to Mark Adams, Chloe and a friend/teammate were off to seven weeks of training with none other than the Yoda of ice hockey himself, the legendary Paul Vincent.

I went to watch her skate after a couple of weeks; and I was blown away by the improvement in her skill, her performance, and the fire I could see coming back in her. I also got to meet Paul Vincent. Italian, in his seventies, he's won a Stanley Cup, an NCAA National Championship, and a state high school championship as a coach; and yes, I readily admit, I was more than a little star-struck when I shook his hand. He's a true gentleman, who still laces up his skates and is on the ice coaching for ten hours a day. He has a very distinctive teaching style, and he gets results.

"I can't believe the difference you've made in my daughter in two weeks," I told him.

He smiled. "Wait 'til you see her at the end of seven weeks."

He made me so comfortable I couldn't resist adding, "I really can't thank you enough for what you've done for her. This is so important for her, especially now, you have no idea." I was getting choked up, thinking of how, a few months ago, she'd left a game and stood crying in the locker room. And now, here she was, getting priceless therapy by grinding it out at the sport she loved.

"Please," he said. "You're a doctor. It's not like I'm saving anyone's life here."

Oh, my God. "I think you probably know what happened to her father, so actually, Paul, you *are* saving her life."

Paul Vincent has become one of the most influential people in her life, along with her Lawrenceville coach, Nicole Uliasz, and our dear friend Olympic ice hockey star Shelley Looney—all three of them gifted coaches and educators who understand that they're not just there to teach a sport, they're there to teach life lessons. They develop the whole person, not just the athlete. They work on the body and the spirit. They came into Chloe's world at the perfect time and helped her heal, and I'll always be indebted to them.

I felt good that my children had a new home they were excited about, and that they were off to London and Cape Cod pursuing their dreams. I have to admit, though, that being alone in that apartment while they were gone made for a fragile, difficult several weeks for me. Dr. Simring had told me to expect the grieving process to get worse before it got better, and she was right. Maybe the numbness was wearing off, like anesthesia, and really exposing the pain. Maybe it was being by myself in a place where we hadn't had a chance to create any memories yet. Maybe it was just starting to sink in, what I knew all too well intellectually but hadn't completely grasped emotionally—Rob wasn't coming back, by his own choice, and there was nothing I could do or say or accomplish or negotiate or pray for that could make that not true. He chose to die. I didn't. So now what?

I grew up fifteen minutes outside New York City. I went to college in New York City, and worked there. I had lots of friends in the city. My brother lived less than twenty-five blocks away, and my dad lived even closer. I could call or text any number of people I loved and make plans in the blink of an eye, but oddly, for me, I didn't feel like being with anyone. Olivia, one of my suicide-survivor girlfriends, had predicted I might not have as much energy for doing things as I used to; and that perfectly described me during those long, empty weeks. I went to work, I saw Dr. Simring, who assured me my grief was proceeding normally, and I headed home to be by myself.

In a dazzling display of bad timing, several men started asking me out. Thanks to the press, I was, after all, famously available and still on television several times a week. These men were amazing, accomplished, kind, and respectful, with even a few celebrities thrown in who owned their own planes. It didn't matter. I had no interest, not one shred. I couldn't even remember what it felt like to be interested. Despite a few tiny pieces having fallen back into place in the previous weeks, I was still shattered. It was all I could do to make sense of myself. The last thing on my mind was trying to make sense of someone else, even if he had his own plane.

The smallest, most well-intentioned comments could set me back. Our building super was, and is, a great guy. He'd gone out of his way to help during the move-in, and one day I thanked him for being so kind and making it so much easier than it could have been.

He shrugged it off with a modest, "I know what happened. I'm glad I could help."

Whether it should have or not, it felt like a little punch in the stomach, another one of those times when I wondered if there were anyone on this planet who didn't know what happened, if my kids and I could ever look forward to some semblance of privacy again or if this dark cloud was just going to follow us around forever. It was also one of those times when I let myself feel more anger than compassion toward Rob. Whoever's fault it was, whoever was to blame, whatever demons he fought for however long, the bottom line was, Rob chose to end his life. We didn't choose to end ours. We didn't ask for this. So why should my kids and I have to serve a life sentence dealing with the consequences of what he did?

I'm a Taurus. I can have a temper. If someone waves a red flag in front of these horns, watch out. I've also always had a long fuse. It takes a lot to use it up, but once that happens, I'll detonate, you can count on it.

But suddenly I found myself in Dr. Simring's office trying to deal with yet another facet of myself that I couldn't recognize for the life of me—after months of what felt like catatonic numbness, that long fuse I'd always counted on had grown much, much shorter. I didn't like it. I didn't like snapping at people. I didn't like my instant impatience with things that weren't really all that important. And I certainly didn't like the idea of this "new me" I was trying to reconstruct being someone who made everyone around me feel as if they had to walk on eggshells.

I gave Dr. Simring a couple of recent examples of times I'd unexpectedly exploded. To the first one she said, "Actually, that was perfectly appropriate." To the second one she said, "Yes, that was definitely a short fuse."

Was it misdirected anger at Rob? Was it that the people

who were closest to me had been so kind for the past few months that my temper had just been taking a breather? What the hell was going on, and what the hell could I do about it?

Dr. Simring reminded me what we'd discussed so often—that suicide is a unique, complex kind of grief; that it inevitably includes anger; and that the only way to heal from it is to let yourself experience it. In my case, the core of this short fuse was actually a vulnerability I was feeling that was completely foreign to me. My insistence on perfection all my life had come with an aversion to "imperfections" like weakness, pain, failure, and self-doubt; and now here I was, being hit out of nowhere with all of those "flaws" at once, without a clue how to protect myself from them. Vulnerable. Exposed. As if for the first time ever, at the age of forty-eight, I was working without the net I'd so carefully constructed for myself as a child. A stranger to myself, and impatient with my inability to just get over it and move on to more important things like, oh, being a solo parent to my kids, for example, which I never expected in a million years, which should never have happened. . . .

So this short-fuse thing was a vulnerability issue. Part of the grieving process, part of the healing process. The remedy for it wasn't "out there," it was "in here." I still had a long way to go, and I needed to be more patient with myself about the journey. It made sense to me. I got it. I didn't like it, but I got it. And if it was the only way to heal, then okay, bring it on.

Obviously it wasn't just Alex, Chloe, and me who'd lost Rob, and when they were back from London and Cape Cod we decided we should have a memorial service for him so that his closest friends could say good-bye. Alex and Chloe did all the planning, from the guest list to the music to the menu. I just arranged for the venue, with the help of an old college boyfriend of mine named Danny Abrams, who kindly offered us the back room of one of his great restaurants, the Mermaid Inn in New York City.

It was a small, intimate gathering of about thirty people, and Alex and Chloe nailed it. It was exactly what Rob would have wanted—delicious food cooked to perfection, stories about him told by his best friends, not even a hint of religion, no sad or somber music, just plenty of love and laughter and a few unavoidable tears, a positive celebration of how he lived, and what an impact he made on so many people, without a single mention of how he died.

I think the kids and I expected it to lift us up, like a kind of upbeat emotional exhale. Instead, to our surprise, as hard as we tried to get into the celebratory spirit in the room, we found ourselves crying. We loved the intention, we loved the people who came, and we loved that we'd made sure it happened; but my God, did we hate what prompted it.

After everyone had gone home we did take a moment to thank Rob for the millionth time for his aversion to funerals. If his memorial service upset us this much, they'd have had to carry us out of his funeral on gurneys.

CHAPTER FOUR

D R. SIMRING HAD WARNED ME THAT MILESTONES WERE GO-ing to be painful, that they would dredge up memories whether I was ready for them or not and make Rob's absence even more glaring than it already was. "It's normal, it's an essential part of healing, and it will hurt," she told me. "The only way to the other side of the pain is through it, not around it, so you have to just let yourself feel it and trust that someday it really will get better."

Dr. Simring was right. That September day came when Alex and Chloe were starting back to school, and it made me ache. Even after Rob and I separated, sending our kids off to their fall semester was something we always did together. He should have been there.

From the time they were in elementary school, Alex and Chloe turned to their dad when they wanted to talk about their classes, their teachers, their homework, what they were reading, which subjects they liked, which subjects they didn't—anything and everything about school was Rob's department, not mine. They loved his sincere, enthusiastic interest in that part of their lives, and he loved being so involved.

I, on the other hand, was what I guess you could call the opposite of a helicopter mom. My thinking was that my children were spending five days a week with professional educators. I trusted those educators to teach my children, and I trusted my children to do what those educators told them to do. I was too busy with two full-time careers to hover over them and be their homework monitor. I remember telling Alex one night, "I already did sixth grade, and I did it pretty well. Now it's your turn to do sixth grade pretty well. You do your job, I'll do mine, your teachers will do theirs, and we'll all be happy."

Alex was already settled into his dorm at Columbia as I finished helping Chloe move into her room at Lawrenceville, which she decorated with lots of photos of Rob. Not until I was driving back to Manhattan did the full force of my anxiety slam into me. Oh, my God—a new school year, and Alex and Chloe's dad, their sidekick and confidant when it came to this kind of thing, was gone. *Really* gone. As in forever. As in never coming back. All they had was the mom who'd always luxuriated in knowing their other parent would deal with it, and I was scared to death of not being able to fill that huge void for them.

I was a solo parent. Not a single parent as far as I was concerned. *Single parent* implies that the other parent is around somewhere. Even if the two parents have decided they can't stand the sight of each other anymore, they can still back each other up, cover for each other, and fill in the blanks for each other when it comes to their cocreated children, so that neither of them has to feel as if they're having to do it all. Rob and I had choreographed that dance beautifully for the past twenty years, even after we separated, even after our divorce was finalized. Alex's school events and high school graduation, Chloe's hockey games, parents' weekends, whatever the occasion, chances were Rob and I would both happily show up, together or separately; but if one of us couldn't make it, the other one would move heaven and earth to get there.

So now what, now that it was just me? Yes, my kids were blessed to have grandparents who lived close by, and their uncle, Evan, and Rob's best friends, aka the "three dads" who'd taken over for him when he checked out. But take parents' weekend, for example. Kids don't want stand-ins on parents' weekend, no matter how much they might love those stand-ins. They don't want stand-ins to talk to about their teachers and their upcoming history final and the latest computer program idea they've come up with. And what about the billion or so requisite school forms, and tuition checks, and emergency contacts, and all those other details? I always took care of those things anyway, but now I didn't have a choice. It was me or nobody, right? And "nobody" wasn't an option, nor was disappointing my kids.

I've said it to countless patients and friends who have several children, and I'll say it again—I don't know how they do it. I know what my fill level is. I know when I'm at full capacity, and two children is full capacity for me. If I had three or four, especially as a solo parent, it's a guarantee that I would inadvertently forget to sign at least one of them up for school, or send them off with no transcripts or emergency contacts. And on that particular milestone day, with Alex and Chloe safely settled in at Columbia and Lawrenceville, the perfectionist in me came back to the apartment hyperconscious that the balance Rob and I had established for our family responsibilities when our kids came along was suddenly gone, and, ready or not, I was "working without a net."

I was feeling very alone, very inadequate, and very sad for them that night. I didn't care how old they were, they were my babies, so brave and strong, so young, only seventeen and eighteen when they found themselves having to deal with their father's suicide. I remembered when I was that age. I was a smart, responsible overachiever whose biggest problem was getting a B+ instead of an A on a test. I could no more have handled my father killing himself than I could have blindfolded myself and performed brain surgery. I was right there with my kids every step of the way, and I still couldn't imagine how they were getting through it. I knew Dr. Simring had a lot to do with it. I hoped I was doing enough for them too, and not letting my own grief, guilt, and blame cloud my vision of what they needed and what more I could do.

Dr. Simring had told me about a concept called "complicated grief." Complicated grief happens when people delay getting help after a terrible trauma, which allows the trauma to become so ingrained and intrusive, like a neglected wound, that the grief process doesn't progress as time goes on, and it becomes more difficult to treat. I was getting help, thanks to therapy. I was back at work, at both my careers, not just going through the motions of them but involved and invested. I wasn't a candidate for complicated grief, was I? I had to be as physically and emotionally healthy as possible for Alex and Chloe now that I was the only parent they had. And a lot of other people, from my patients to my coworkers at ABC to my viewers, were counting on me too.

The one thing I hadn't done was to reach out to other suicide survivors I didn't know, who'd be objective with me, to find out how they got through it, if they'd experienced the same struggles and self-doubts I was having, and if they'd found ways to make peace with all the unanswerable questions suicide leaves in its wake. Maybe new perspectives from other people who'd been there would give me more clarity and strength than I was feeling. Maybe other survivors were the answer to, "What more can I do to heal for my kids?" There was only one way to find out.

I'd received an e-mail from a woman named "Sarah Davies." (At her request, I'm using an alias for her.) Sarah was only seventeen, my children's age, when she lost a parent to suicide—in this case, her mother—many years ago.

Her e-mail read, in part, "Back in 1976, therapy was not even considered, so I spent decades trying to make sense of it all and feeling tremendous shame over the tragedy." Seventeen, at a time when, for the most part, therapy was reserved for profound mental illness, trying to heal from her mother's suicide with no one there to guide her through it. I couldn't imagine it.

I called her, and she generously told me her story, a story that continues to haunt me and inspire me to this day.

Sarah was born and raised in Manhattan, in what she describes as "not a loving, supportive home." She and her brother, two years older, grew up with a nanny while her parents partied their way through the 1960s, not especially involved or interested in their children's lives. Her brother coped with their absence by becoming an introvert who mostly stayed in his room. Sarah coped by becoming very independent. She had a lot of freedom and a lot of friends, and she spent the majority of her time at their houses rather than be alone with a nanny and an unavailable brother in an emotionally indifferent home.

Sarah's parents divorced when she was thirteen. Her father moved to California, and her brother was sent off to a boarding school called Blair Academy. Her mom remarried and found herself with an emotionally abusive new husband, a writer who happened to be gifted at using words to either charm or decimate his wife, depending on which suited him better at any given moment. Sarah stayed as absent as she always had, enjoying her friends and her high school years at Fieldston.

Predictably, her mother's second marriage didn't last long. Her mom was deeply traumatized when she and her husband separated. She hated the thought of being alone, and she quickly started dating again.

And then, over Christmas break in 1975, Sarah's mom took her and her brother to her house in Remsenburg, New York, and it was as if a whole new mother had shown up. The three of them played in the snow, took lots of pictures, and just hung out together and had fun. Her mom was suddenly asking questions, taking an interest in Sarah's life and trying to get to know her. It was a first for Sarah, and it felt great. She had no idea what brought it on; but whatever it was, she came home from that trip excited and hopeful that maybe, at the age of seventeen, she'd finally become engaging enough to attract her mother's attention.

A month later, on January 24, 1976, Sarah got home from a date with her boyfriend at around 1:00 A.M. On her way to her room she noticed in passing that her mom's bedroom door was slightly open, and the lights were on. Her mom was on a date that night too, and it was unusual for her to be out so late. But Sarah shrugged it off and went on to bed. As she fell asleep she pulled the covers tightly around her and wondered why it was so cold in the house.

She was startled awake a couple of hours later by loud

pounding at the front door. She blearily answered it to find the police standing there, grim and abrupt.

"Miss," one of them said, "we have some very bad news for you—your mom apparently jumped out of a window in this apartment and killed herself." Sarah and her mother lived on the fifteenth floor of the building. The doorman had found the violently shattered body on the sidewalk and called the cops. He'd managed to identify the deceased and directed the cops to Sarah's apartment door.

Sarah immediately went numb with shock, unable to even take this news in, let alone process it. She was all by herself in that empty apartment, with no one there to comfort her or take charge. In a daze she made her way to her mother's room. No wonder it was so cold in the house—it was winter in New York City, and the window was wide open.

She looked around. There was no note. No apology, no explanation, almost no memories to speak of . . . except that last Christmas. Is this what that was about? Had she already started planning this a month ago, and that was her way of saying good-bye?

It was as if Sarah had been abducted out of a sound sleep into some alternate reality. Suicide was as foreign to her as life on Mars. She'd never met or even heard of anyone who'd killed themselves, and her surreal haze was an overwhelming combination of grief and shame. Who does this?! Whose *mother* does this?!

Her memories of the next few weeks are very vague, but she knows that her father and brother arrived, and that her father initiated an investigation. Sarah's mom had been a gorgeous, sexy, sophisticated woman. Neither he nor any of her friends could imagine that she would choose such a disfiguring way to kill herself.

According to the investigators, she'd had a phone conversation that evening with her second, estranged husband; and he may or may not have laid a guilt trip on her about her date that night. Earlier in the week, she'd gone to her doctor, who put her on an antidepressant. So little was known about mental illness and depression in the mid-1970s, let alone about the appropriate drugs to treat them, that it was anyone's guess what effect the medication might have had on her. And there was some indication that she might have had a glass of wine before she went out that night, which could have interacted very badly with whatever that antidepressant was.

In the end, there was no indication that anyone else was involved in Sarah's mom's death. It was ruled a suicide. Case closed.

Sarah didn't get involved in the investigation, or in the busywork and arrangements that had to be dealt with. She left that to the adults; and they were so preoccupied with their own grief and logistics that she and her brother were pretty much on their own when it came to sorting out the impossible tidal wave of sorrow, confusion, guilt, and anger that "come with the meal" in the aftermath of suicide. All the familiar questions swirled around in her head: Did she just not matter? Would it have made a difference if she'd stayed home that night? Or been a better daughter? Did she miss signs that this was coming? She was seventeen years old and not that close to her mom. Where was everyone else who should have known what signs to look for and knew her mom better than she did? What about that doctor who gave her those pills? Did he notice anything? And what were those pills, anyway? Were they safe, or were they what drove her mom out the window on that freezing cold night?

Endless questions, and no one to help her answer them or sort them out. She hadn't seen much of her dad after the divorce, so there she was with a father she really didn't know all that well. He did try—he arranged for Sarah's older half brother to come to New York and stay in his apartment with her until she graduated from Fieldston in June. But beyond that, he was basically at a loss and headed back to California the minute he'd fulfilled his obligations.

Sarah did successfully graduate and go on to college at the University of California, Santa Barbara. She dealt with her flood of powerful emotions by not dealing with them, afraid that if she let herself start feeling them she'd never stop, and they'd pull her under. She kept everything light and had fun with her friends, and if anyone asked about her mother, she'd lie and say, "Mom died in a car crash."

At the same time, she was painfully aware of all the feelings she was masking, and how much her mother's suicide was defining her. Underneath the facade of a happy young woman doing well at school was a young woman who felt deeply ashamed and privately different, hiding a terrible secret from everyone around her. If people found out her mother had killed herself, they might look at her with pity, which would be unbearable; or she might be exposed as such an unworthy, unlovable person that not even her own mom found her worth sticking around for. Her mom had dealt her the ultimate rejection, and she must have deserved it or it wouldn't have happened.

It took ten years, but Sarah found her way to therapy. She was finally able to come out of hiding, tell the truth about what happened to her mother, and start unraveling the decade of unaddressed feelings she'd never opened up about before without worrying about judgment or blame. She started working with her father in the family TV advertising business; and she was in the process of getting her master's degree in social work at the University of Southern California, pursuing her dream of working with orphaned children and adolescents.

Then, in 1993, Sarah was blindsided again, by the death of her father. As she put it, she "grieved like there was no tomorrow." And as she grieved, she realized that she wasn't just grieving her father—for the first time, she was grieving her mother too. She and I had such a good talk about how odd it seems that we don't get better at loss as we suffer more of it in our lives. Instead, the losses seem to accumulate, and compound each other. Just as Sarah didn't fully grieve her mother's suicide until her father passed away, I didn't fully grieve my divorce from Rob until I was grieving his suicide. I'm sure it's like, on a much, much smaller scale, the skin being sensitized by a bad sunburn. The pain seems to go away as the sunburn heals, but even the slightest touch can still hurt like hell, far more than it ever would have if the sunburn had never happened in the first place.

Sarah was in her second year at USC when her father died. After much soul-searching, she left her social work dream behind and took over the family business, which had just celebrated its sixtieth anniversary.

Sarah had gotten married in 1989 and had two beautiful boys. She remembers the sadness that overcame her sometimes as she rocked them, feeling a sacred, unconditional connection with them, a mother's love, deeper than any love she'd ever felt in her life. Had her mother ever felt that love for her, even for a moment? And if she had, how on earth could she have chosen to leave her? How was that possible?

Those thoughts led to a conscious, deliberate decision on her part. Instead of living what she'd known, following the path she'd learned as a child and being an absent, distant mom, she let her childhood teach her what *not* to do. She made a vow to herself and her sons: She was going to stick around for her boys for as long as humanly possible, no matter what, and be the best mom she could possibly be, the loving, involved mom she wished she'd had. It was a choice, *her* choice, inspired by lessons she'd learned the hard way from her mother, without anger or resentment. In fact, she felt a surge of sympathy toward her mom. Sarah and her brother came along when their mom was in her early twenties. Maybe she wasn't ready. Maybe she was overwhelmed, or depressed, or emotionally unequipped to be a young mother. Maybe she was too burdened to experience the peace and the pure joy Sarah felt when she rocked her babies to sleep. How sad, if that were true. What a loss, maybe even more for their mom than for Sarah and her brother. And now, of course, she wasn't even there to ask.

Another big step toward resolving her resentment toward her mother came from Sarah's faith. She was raised Jewish, but she married a devout Christian; and they decided together to raise their boys in the Christian Church. Sarah dutifully attended services with her husband and children to be supportive, and gradually the messages of resurrection, eternal life, hope, God's love, and forgiveness began to resonate in her soul. She was baptized in 2011, when she and her husband separated and she found herself reliving the same abandonment issues she'd gone through with her mother's suicide—the blame, the shame, the guilt, the what-ifs, the rock-bottom *Why wasn't I enough?* of a failing marriage. But her newfound faith and her love for her sons and her family and friends saw her through it.

It was around the time of her divorce in 2015 that Sarah had an epiphany that was a giant, unexpected step toward healing. She was by herself, at the beach, deeply depressed and in such enormous emotional pain that she found herself thinking, "I don't want to do this anymore." All she'd have to do, she realized, was just walk into the ocean and keep walking, and the pain would be over.

In the end, of course, she didn't do it. She couldn't do it. But at that profoundly low moment in her life it hit her that her mother must have felt exactly the same way when she killed herself, but on steroids, multiplied to infinity. During Sarah's "I don't want to do this anymore" she completely blocked out any thoughts of her children, her friends, her successful career, all the blessings in her life, and for the first time she got it, really *got it*, that her mom's suicide had absolutely nothing to do with her. For the first time, she was finally able to let go of the guilt, shame, blame, feelings of rejection and abandonment, and not only be happy for her mother that she was at peace and not suffering anymore but actually forgive her with all her heart. "Be kind to one another, tenderhearted, forgiving one another, as God in Christ forgave you" (Ephesians 4:32).

Sarah looks back on her journey through the aftermath of suicide with enormous gratitude. It was rough, often excruciating, but she now considers herself a world-class survivor who can get through anything. She's developed the gifts of empathy, compassion, and a depth she's not sure she would have had if she hadn't been forced to take this journey; and she's very well aware of the perspective she's gained over all these years about what matters and what doesn't. She loves and accepts love fearlessly, having lived through one of the worst things that can possibly happen and chosen to let it lead her to peaceful insight rather than bitterness. The resilience of the human spirit never ceases to amaze her, a fact she tries to exemplify to her sons every day as they make their way through their twenties.

Sarah also thinks of her mom every day even now, with a realization she never thought possible: while suicide is definitely a part of her and always will be, it no longer defines her.

Sarah's story was more helpful to me than I ever imagined it could be. Her strength and determination to survive after such a terrible trauma at such a young age bolstered me. Her experience with complicated grief, circumstantial as it was, reminded me that trying to bury pain in a lot of denial and busyness instead of addressing it doesn't heal that pain, it only postpones it and gives it the power to blindside you when it inevitably catches up with you.

Perhaps most of all, though, it encouraged me to tap into a whole new resource for support—the vast community of suicide survivors who'd been where Alex and Chloe and I were, the people who'd already navigated the rough journey we still had ahead of us, a journey I dreaded.

CHAPTER FIVE

MILESTONE NUMBER TWO, A HUGE ONE, CAME RIGHT ON the heels of my kids heading back to school. The end of September brought Yom Kippur, the Jewish Day of Atonement and the holiest day of the year in Judaism.

I was raised Jewish. My Italian mother converted to Judaism when she married my dad. I've always considered myself more of a cultural Jew than a religious one—I went to temple maybe two or three times a year, and the Jewish holidays I enthusiastically celebrated were the ones that involved family meals.

Rob wasn't Jewish. In fact, he wasn't religious at all. I didn't disrespect that, or think I had any business trying to dictate his beliefs. So I didn't argue when, especially in the last ten years or so of our marriage, he completely stopped going to temple with me on holidays. But I admit, at the same time, I resented his refusal to at least go through the motions on occasions that were so much about family. I'd sit there by myself, or sometimes with Alex and/or Chloe, on Rosh Hashana and Yom Kippur and wonder what it would be like to have a partner who wanted to be there just because it was important to me.

When Alex and Chloe and I moved into our Manhattan apartment, we joined the reform congregation that Evan and his wife, Tanya, had just joined. I loved the idea of observing the High Holy Days with my family, especially the Yizkor memorial service of Yom Kippur, when we mourn our deceased loved ones. I'd be mourning Rob in public for the first time, and it was a great comfort to know that I wouldn't be sitting there alone, surrounded by a synagogue full of bereaved strangers.

Alex went with friends to a service at Columbia. Chloe came up from Lawrenceville, and we met Evan and Tanya at the temple. They were already seated, Evan to Tanya's left in the pew. I slid in beside Tanya, with Chloe sitting on my right.

Yom Kippur had been a very emotional day for me for the past twelve years or so, a day to join thousands of other mourners to remember and celebrate the lives of people we'd loved and lost—in my case, my father's second wife, Iggy, with whom I'd been very close; my mother's best friend, Claire; and my godmother, Marianne. Tanya was mourning her father, who'd been killed in a tragic car accident two years to the day before Rob's suicide. Now we were formally adding Rob to the list. This was going to be excruciating.

Tanya already had a small mountain of Kleenex ready on the pew beside her. For reasons no one including me can explain, I never have Kleenex in my apartment, so I'd brought toilet paper instead, pulled it out of my purse, and added it to Tanya's tissue supply. It helped me to have Tanya there, and I wondered if it helped her to have me there. Here we were, side by side, two women who were juggling careers, family, and the fresh, raw pain of sudden death. I felt more connected to her than I ever had before and marveled at how, without a word being said, the shared experience of grief can draw people closer together. No wonder this particular service of Yom Kippur is so treasured. No matter how alone someone might feel when they walk through the doors of the temple, they know they're not alone when they leave.

I was holding up marginally well until Evan quietly stood up and sidestepped his way past his wife and me and took his seat on the other side of Chloe. That's when I lost it and burst into a major tearfest—there was something so powerful, and heartbreaking, and tender about seeing my brother moving to comfort his niece, my daughter, who was there to mourn her father, who could have and should have still been alive.

Suddenly, out of nowhere, among the heightened emotions that were churning around inside me, a flash of anger rose to the surface. I usually tried to push my anger away when it came to Rob, because it seemed so disrespectful and made me feel guilty. But not then, not on Yom Kippur, not sitting next to my devastated daughter on a holiday that was already so important and emotionally complicated for me. Rob gave up coming with me for this occasion when he was alive, when maybe I just needed someone to sit beside me and hold my hand, no matter what he believed or didn't believe. Oh, well. His choice. Now he wasn't here because he wasn't alive, and it was my brother's arm around our daughter to comfort her, not his, not her father's. Oh, well. Again, his choice. He probably would have even thought it was ridiculous that we were sitting in a religious memorial service crying over him. Oh, well, Rob. *Our* choice.

Yizkor isn't just for mourning people we've personally lost. It's also for mourning people we as a community have lost. It's somber, it's quiet, and there's a sacred, communal energy in the air that intensifies the prayers for the memory of the departed; and at that particular service we were also mourning our cantor's husband, who'd died of cancer less than a month earlier. But there she was, leading that massive congregation while going through her own grief. Her poised courage sent me into a whole new wave of tears.

I looked around in the stillness of the service at the thousand or so congregants, wondering who each of them was crying for; what each of their hearts was going through; if anyone else had lost someone to suicide and was having occasional pangs like I was, that the death I was grieving was different, maybe not quite as legitimate or worthy of all this reverence as everyone else's. Did they feel a little set apart like I did, and a little ashamed? Were any of these people looking at me and wondering if I should even be there at all, since they could have heard about Rob on the news and, if I was suddenly remembering correctly, suicide was considered a violation of Jewish law?

I was accustomed to leaving the Yom Kippur memorial service emotionally drained. I left this one emotionally drained times a million, very unsettled, and hating the feeling.

I simmered about it for a while, and then finally I got in touch with a man I'd been hearing about who might be able to give me some peace of mind. His name is Rabbi David-Seth Kirshner. He happened to be the local rabbi at my old synagogue many years back, Temple Emanu-El, in Closter, New Jersey. I'd never met him, but by all accounts he was articulate, charismatic, and, amazingly, a passionate advocate for destigmatizing mental illness and suicide in the wake of the suicide of his brother.

I quickly discovered he was all those things and more, when he kicked off our conversation by telling me about his first sermon to his new congregants at Temple Emanu-El for the High Holy Days. It began something like, "I'm going to share something with you that's heartfelt and passionate and honest, and I hope it's taken that way—my brother Gabriel died by suicide ten years ago, and I want to tell you about him and his life."

I was glad we were on the phone so he couldn't see my

jaw drop open. I applauded his courage for being so open about it, especially as a rabbi in front of a group of strangers. He shrugged off the compliment.

"Actually," he said, "I hadn't planned it ahead of time, but I look back on it as one of the healthiest things I've ever done." For one thing, he wasn't about to play into the stigma, make excuses for his brother's death and worry about the truth of the suicide coming out before he was ready. As he put it, "This is about a mental illness. This is about a death. This isn't a marketing decision." For another thing, he wanted to introduce himself to his congregants as more human than divine. "If I'm going to be your rabbi, I want you to know right up front that I've gone through shit too, just like you've gone through shit. Whether it's cancer, or financial disaster, or a family crisis—whatever you've got, I've got stuff too, and you can come talk to me about anything."

Rabbi Kirshner is the youngest of four boys in a close-knit family. Their father was a rabbi, and their mother was a homemaker and courtroom stenographer. In 1975, the eldest son, Gabriel, thirteen years older than Rabbi Kirshner and academically gifted, went off to the Talmudical Academy, an all-boys modern Orthodox yeshiva outside of Baltimore, Maryland, to begin the eighth grade. Their parents were uneasy about sending their child away to school, but the guidance counselor, Rabbi Ephraim Shapiro, befriended them and promised to look after Gabe.

Rabbi Kirshner remembers him, his brothers, and his parents kissing and hugging Gabriel good-bye and heading back to their home in Pottstown, Pennsylvania.

It was, as far as the family was concerned, the last time they saw Gabe. When he came home to visit, he was a different person. He was angry and violent, quick to cry, inappropriate, and refusing any and all physical affection. After his first year at the yeshiva he begged not to go back. His parents wondered about the change in him, and about his literally pleading not to be sent back to Baltimore; and they hoped that by letting him stay home and go to public school with his three brothers he'd return to his old self again.

Rabbi Kirshner learned to walk on eggshells around him like the rest of the family did. At times he was embarrassed and ashamed that Gabe was weird and that other people made fun of him.

Then, when he was around twenty-five years old, Gabriel seemed to find his way again. He joined the Air Force, graduated from college with honors, fell in love and got married, and signed up for rabbinical school. He was still odd and quirky, but the rabbinate welcomed him, and he earned his ordination. He got a job, he and his wife had a beautiful baby girl, and the family was relieved, happy for him and proud of him.

Then, seemingly out of nowhere, Gabriel, at the age of thirty-six, went into a tailspin. His job became more than he could handle, his marriage was falling apart, and his behavior was becoming more and more erratic and extreme. And then came July 17, 1996.

Rabbi Kirshner was in Israel, leading a tour group of sixty-five teenagers, when he was summoned to an emergency phone call. TWA Flight 800 had crashed into the Atlantic that day near East Moriches, New York, and the rabbi hurried to the nearest phone, afraid that one of the kids' parents was on that plane.

Instead, Rabbi Kirshner was told to call home immediately. As he listened to the phone ring at his parents' house, he convinced himself that whichever parent answered the phone, the other one must be dead. He wasn't even slightly prepared when they both answered and said, "Gabriel committed suicide."

In the process of telling me this story, he gave me a perfect description for that moment when the Port Authority detective told me Rob had jumped off the George Washington Bridge and killed himself:

"It's like you're walking down the street on a nice day in Manhattan, the sun is shining, everything's right in your world, and someone on the top floor of the apartment building you're passing pours boiling hot water out the window and it hits you. Your first reaction is, 'What the hell . . . ?!' Your second reaction is, 'Oh, my God!' And then it just starts to hurt, and create boils, welts, and pain beyond description."

That was it exactly.

It seems that on a day when Gabriel's wife left town on a six-hour trip, he climbed into his car in his closed garage, ran a garden hose from the exhaust into the car, and poisoned himself with carbon monoxide. By the time his wife got home and found him, it was estimated by the medical examiner that Gabe had been dead in the car for three to four hours. Despite that evidence to the contrary, his father clung to the belief for the rest of his life that Gabriel chose carbon monoxide as his manner of suicide in the hope that someone would walk in on him and stop him in time.

Rabbi Kirshner was the only one in his family who wasn't married yet, so he was the one who volunteered to go to California, where Gabriel lived and died, to pack up Gabe's widow and their two-year-old daughter and move them back to Detroit. He remembers it as one of the most horrible times in his life.

And remarkably, especially in 1996, the family decided they were never going to hide the cause of Gabriel's death like so many other families routinely did. There would be no "heart attack," no "car accident," no "natural causes." Gabriel killed himself. That was the truth, and if they could figure out a way to live with it, the rest of the world damned well could too.

Like every other suicide survivor, Rabbi Kirshner fell into a reaction pattern he came to call SARA, i.e., shock, anger, resentment, and acceptance; and over time he came to believe that we survivors volley back and forth between guilt and blame to soothe ourselves and then punish ourselves. He and his family went through the usual agonizing process of what-ifs and if-onlys, looking for answers to all the unanswerable questions about what caused Gabriel to take his own life. They began "unpacking his baggage," almost like forensic investigators, to put the puzzle of Gabe's life back together and learn more about him, in search of that moment or that event that could give them the "aha!" they so desperately wanted.

It took ten years, but they finally unearthed a heartbreaking piece of information about Gabriel they'd never known before—while Gabe was at the Talmudical Academy, the kind, protective guidance counselor, Rabbi Ephraim Shapiro, who'd befriended Rabbi Kirshner's parents and promised to look out for his brother, sexually molested hundreds of boys at the academy. In 2007, after major exposé articles came out about Rabbi Shapiro in *The Forward* and *The Jewish Week*, Rabbi Kirshner started reaching out to Gabe's classmates, and they confirmed that, yes, Gabe was one of Rabbi Shapiro's victims. Apparently the only person Gabe had confided in about the molestation was a doctor he'd seen for psychoanalysis. He never told his wife, and he certainly never told anyone in the family.

Suddenly, finally, they had someone and something to blame for Gabriel's suicide—for a minute. But once this discovery had a chance to settle in, Rabbi Kirshner found himself circling back to the same awful guilt he'd been struggling with before. Gabe hadn't come home from the Talmudical Academy the same happy-go-lucky boy he and his parents had dropped off, and he'd begged not to go back for a second year. They'd obviously been too naïve to make the connection and left the changes in him at a simple "different." In the end, who cared if it was the trauma of molestation or fifty other things that caused a severe enough depression to compel him to take his own life? Rabbi Shapiro reportedly victimized hundreds of boys while he was at the academy. If that was the direct cause of Gabe's suicide, then wouldn't it stand to reason that those hundreds of other boys would have killed themselves too?

And over time Rabbi Kirshner expanded that logic to his family as well. Gabriel was one of four sons, all of whom grew up in the same household he did. None of the other three had taken their own life. So maybe—probably— suicide is very much like lightning striking, having nothing to do with whether or not you were loved enough or hugged enough as a child. It's infinitely deeper and more complicated than that.

Sadly, in the end, Rabbi Kirshner realized that when his brother was living, he saw him as different. When his brother died, and Rabbi Kirshner learned about his life, he realized he was just very sick. He still kicks himself that he didn't understand that at the time, and he's trying to make up for it now, by becoming an outspoken advocate for therapy, and for destigmatizing and shining a light on how pervasive and indiscriminating mental illness is in our society. Nearly every family in his congregation is dealing with some mental instability or other, and he reminds his children all the time that "Everyone's got something." He values therapy in his own life and openly admits that he gets depressed himself, but therapy is his way of staying out in front of it.

As he put it in one of our conversations, which made me smile because I don't doubt it for a moment, "So many of my congregants watch everything they put in their mouths and work out six times a week, but they make no effort at all to tend to their mental health."

He's also noticed, time and time again, that when someone in his synagogue community is diagnosed with a serious physical illness like cancer, the whole community mobilizes, volunteering to transport the kids to and from school, run household errands, deliver meals to the family, take turns being with the cancer patient during their chemotherapy treatments, and drive them to doctors' appointments—whatever they can do to help, they're right there, full of active compassion without a moment of hesitation. He strongly suspects, though, that if the diagnosis were depression, or bipolar disorder, or OCD, or any other mental illness, that same community would probably whisper about it to one another and keep their distance, rather than make it their business to learn what to do and how to help.

In fact, he wrote a wonderful blog called "Mental Illness Is Not the 'Cooties'" that included a "to-do" list for how communities could and should deal with mental illness. With his permission, I'm quoting that list, since I could never do it justice by paraphrasing it:

- Don't whisper about mental illness. The strides that were achieved by the LGBTQ community came as a result of people being bold enough to come out and share their identity and story. We have embraced breast cancer with pink ribbons, annual walks, and a month of pink end zones in the NFL. So too do we have to "come out" about mental illness and embrace those who are stricken. Drawing near to those with health challenges and making Google spreadsheets for meals and carpools are no less important for the person suffering from depression than they are for the person receiving chemo. Sicknesses might present differently but being ill takes us all off our game and we all can stand to benefit from help. That comes by being able to say in a full-throated manner that we are sick, battling a mental illness, and need help, or that we are helping someone with a mental illness.
- Mental illness needs a ribbon too. I am not sure what colors are available. Orange is for gun control, purple

is sexual abuse awareness, and yellow is for our soldiers and those MIA. Perhaps gray but it really does not matter as much as being able to wear our awareness on our proverbial sleeve. Let's talk about it more freely and create awareness and support.

- Mental illness is not contagious and we need to stop treating it like the cooties. Do not be afraid to help those in need, get close to them, and be the support they desperately require and will benefit from in this time of need. Equally important, do not wait to be asked to help. Be proactive. [Author and Facebook COO] Sheryl Sandberg says the best support she received after the sudden death of her husband was someone asking her, "What do you NOT want on your hamburger?" Being present will not cure mental illness any more than carpools cure cancer. But the presence and support matter.

- Know the numbers. We are not miracle workers or magicians. We cannot make the disease go away but we can help. Sometimes, the illness needs more resources than a Google spreadsheet can offer. Know the numbers of suicide prevention hotlines. Keep the numbers of accredited psychiatrists near to be able to offer the support that is beyond our grade of expertise. Do not try and wear a cape or offer simple solutions to solve the problem.

And speaking of the LGBTQ community, particularly the teenagers, Rabbi Kirshner is well aware of their elevated anxiety and vulnerability to suicide, and he extends himself to them at every opportunity to give them the message that God loves them just as much as he loves anyone else. Politics aside, it really does take a village. The sad fact is, a lot of parents are ill-equipped to deal with LGBTQ issues, he tells them, but that doesn't mean the whole world is. Their rabbi, their pastor, their doctor, their school counselor, their coach, support hotlines—there are available, understanding resources they can turn to, and it's up to us adults, *all* of us, to do our parts to make sure these kids know they're not alone.

Rabbi Kirshner is encouraged, though, by the progress being made toward a better understanding of mental illness and suicide in Judaism. A hundred years ago, when a Jew committed suicide, they were not to be buried with the rest of the Jewish community. They were buried on the outskirts of the cemetery, to dissuade people from killing themselves, with the added message that mental illness really *is* different from cancer or a heart attack.

The evolution that's taken place is that rabbis of all denominations, even the Orthodox, are finally saying that people who die of suicide are dying of a mental illness; that mental illness is as serious, and as involuntary, an affliction as physical illness; and that we have no more business turning our backs on the mentally ill than we have of turning our backs on someone who suffers from cancer, heart disease, or any other physical malady.

Rabbi Kirshner has found a lot of healing in his advocacy of destigmatizing suicide and mental illness, to honor his brother's memory and spare as many other people as possible the devastating pain Gabriel and their whole family went through. Even after all these years there's still sorrow, and there are still tears—he hasn't found that coping with Gabe's suicide necessarily gets easier, he's just learned to deal with it better, recognize the pain for what it is, and transform it from reactive to proactive every chance he gets.

Not once when we talked, by the way, did Rabbi Kirshner use euphemisms like "when Gabe died" or "when Gabe passed away." It was always "when Gabe killed himself" or "when Gabe took his life." Even in private conversations, he won't buy into the stigma. As I told him, that's something I still needed to work on.

Gabe's suicide caused major changes in the family. It was the only time in his life Rabbi Kirshner ever saw his usually stoic father cry; and when he spoke at his father's funeral he said, "My father's heart stopped beating today, but he died fifteen years ago, on July 17, 1996."

For the rest of the family, though, it was a reboot, a heightened awareness of how fragile life is and a determination to act like it that's still true today. They'd always been close. Gabriel's death brought them even closer. They don't fight. They don't harbor grudges. They talk to each other every day. They go out of their way to make sure Gabe's daughter is tethered to their side of the family. They never miss family reunions. They never end a phone call without saying, "I love you." And Rabbi Kirshner has made it his personal mission to try every single day to have the same relationship with his children and living siblings that he would love to have had with his brother.

One of the most valuable gifts he feels his brother left him is a crystal clarity about priorities, which includes zero tolerance for drama and pettiness. I told him about the conversations I'd been having with Dr. Simring about the "short fuse" I'd been experiencing, and he shared the message he ingrains in his congregants, and lives as well: "Life is too short to sweat the small stuff. Invest your energy in the things and the people that matter. Other than that, cut the crap."

Who could argue with that? And who knew I'd come away from conversations with a respected, widely renowned rabbi wanting to needlepoint "Cut the Crap" on a pillow? Talking to him shined the most refreshing spotlight on how much of what I used to get worked up about boiled down to nothing but "crap," and how I was starting to realize that in the overall scope of things, most of it couldn't matter less. I hate being late, for example. My blood pressure would soar if traffic or something else beyond my control would get in my way and make it happen. Now? I still hate being late, but if I can't do anything about it, oh, well, it's better than not getting there at all, and it's stopped even registering on my stress meter. I used to panic if a bit of makeup would get onto my top when I was about to go on national television. Now? If a little makeup ends up on my top and a viewer notices, I just take it as a compliment that they're paying such close attention. I missed a flight once. Completely my fault, by the way. You would have thought it was the most horrible crisis since the stock market crash of 2008. Now? I've cut it close a few times and find myself thinking, "If I miss this flight, I'll just catch the next one. Or not." Rabbi Kirshner was exactly right—"cut the crap" is a very liberating way to live.

I hung up after our conversation inspired, comforted, humbled by his outspoken courage and activism, and more than a little overwhelmed. It was so much to process, when I was still just trying to make it through one day at a time keeping my two jobs and my two kids intact. He'd given me a lot to shoot for, though. Maybe someday I could get there. If only someday didn't seem so far away.

CHAPTER SIX

I N OCTOBER I FOUND MYSELF HAVING TO TACKLE THE MOST brutally difficult physical obligation I'd dealt with since Rob's suicide. People talk about cremation all the time, but I've never heard anyone talk about the excruciating errand that goes along with it. I finally had to pick up Rob's ashes.

The funeral home had called in August with a gentle, respectful reminder that they'd been holding the ashes for six months and were wondering when I'd like to stop by and get them. *Dread* is not too strong a word. The thought of it was horrifying, and I knew I'd never be able to handle it by myself. I immediately picked up the phone and called Michael Asch. There's a reason he's my best friend. Before I even finished asking the question he said, "I'll go with you." I didn't mention a word about it to anyone else, including Alex and Chloe. They would have volunteered to come home from school and go with me. Evan and any number of friends would have volunteered to go with me. But Michael's one of those take-care-of-business friends who never needs an explanation, he just gets it done, no muss, no fuss, no drama; and making him my first call was a no-brainer.

Michael's schedule is as crazy as mine, so the fact that it took us two months to get this awful errand over with wasn't that surprising. To be honest, I'm not sure I could have handled it a minute sooner anyway.

It almost made the whole thing even more obscene that our time at the funeral home was so brief and unceremonious. Michael and I walked in. I identified myself and explained why we were there, and a very few minutes later someone appeared with a bag of ashes that used to be my husband, my children's father, a highly respected thoracic surgeon, a spectacular cook, an avid reader, dog lover, and hockey fan. As this person walked toward me with what used to be Rob, all I could think was, "Never in a million years did I expect this was something I'd have to do. No one should ever have to do this."

The person extended the bag of ashes to me. I didn't say a word, and neither did Michael, he just reached over and took the bag so that I wouldn't have to, and we left. I may or may not have remembered to say thank you—the people at the funeral home were very nice, and this couldn't have been an easy job for them. It wasn't their fault that I couldn't get out of there fast enough, I was just sure that if I'd had to spend one more minute in that place, I would have stopped breathing.

We walked to my car. I was crying. Michael hugged me and set the bag in the car. I drove home so glad I hadn't put Alex and Chloe through this. I would leave it up to them what to do with their dad's ashes when they were ready. When he'd first been cremated they'd thought of scattering them in Maine, on the property of a close friend's house he loved to visit. Then they thought maybe closer to home . . . or not. . . . I reminded them that there was no hurry, they didn't have to decide so soon after his death.

And by the way, I added, trying to lighten things up a little, to avoid this dilemma when my time comes, I wanted each of them to keep half my ashes in an urn or a bag or whatever, in a safe place so they can't be knocked off a mantel or something and make a mess all over the floor. They exchanged an "Is she kidding?" look, followed by Alex saying, "So wherever Chloe and I go for the rest of our lives, we're supposed to move your ashes along with us?"

"Absolutely," I said. "You'll never get rid of me."

It wasn't easy, but I managed to get Rob's ashes from the car to my apartment. They weren't heavy, they were just . . . Rob's ashes. I know. I'm a doctor. An Ob-Gyn. There's not much I haven't seen and held in my hands. And I've been to several funerals in my life. But not once had I ever been faced with actually handling a deceased loved one's remains. I put the bag in my closet and decided not to mention it, or this horrible day, to my kids, at least until they came home for Thanksgiving, if not longer.

They came home for Thanksgiving, and it was too soon to talk about it.

The bag is still in my closet.

Of course, Thanksgiving was another tough milestone. We were having dinner at Evan and Tanya's with their two little boys and my parents. It would be Tanya's third Thanksgiving without her father, and our first without Rob. Since it was a secular holiday and food was heavily involved, Rob *loved* Thanksgiving.

It was also a good reminder to me how much time I waste anticipating things, based on what I think I know for sure. A year earlier, Rob and I were in the process of getting divorced. I'd spent much of that Thanksgiving imagining how we'd handle it once the divorce was final. My parents had had an amicable divorce, even though they didn't like each other that much, and they'd been divorced for almost thirty years by the time Rob and I were ending our marriage. And from day one they put those feelings aside for family holidays and events; so thanks to them, I had the best role models for how blended and post-divorce families could look on special occasions. I'd assumed Rob and I could carry on that tradition and sit down to Thanksgiving dinner together as usual. If not, would we take turns and spend alternate Thanksgivings with Alex and Chloe? Or what if we found significant others? My parents had handled that, I was sure we could too. But what if one of us found a significant other and the other didn't? Me, Alex, Chloe, and some woman watching Rob carve the turkey. Okay, maybe a little weird at first, but we'd make it work. You name it, I pictured it. By the time I was through, I was sure I'd covered every possible scenario. Except one, obviously. Not in my wildest, darkest dreams had I imagined this one. "Man plans, God laughs."

Thanksgiving of 2017 went perfectly well. We started the meal remembering, without naming them, those we loved who were once with us but weren't anymore, and we honored the holiday by acknowledging the many things we had to be grateful for—our family, our health, our prosperity, being together, the beautiful meal, and Evan and Tanya's sons, my six-year-old and two-year-old nephews, who were their own little "no sadness" zones.

It was admittedly a less joyful, more muted gratitude than usual that Thanksgiving, possibly like that of a small group of people whose cruise ship had just gone down who were thanking God that they'd made it to their lifeboat. But it was gratitude nonetheless; and, as always, I thought of our police, our firefighters, our EMTs and all other first responders, and most certainly the men and women in the military who defend our country. My father was a captain in the U.S. Air Force, and I was born on George Air Force Base in California. My respect for the military is immeasurable, and I raised my children never to pass up an opportunity to thank them for their service.

So I was especially moved when, sometime after that Thanksgiving had come and gone, I met a woman named Kim Ruocco. Kim has a BA in Human Services and Psychology from the University of Massachusetts at Amherst and a master's degree in Clinical Social Work from Boston University. She's the Vice President of Suicide Prevention and Postvention for TAPS, the Tragedy Assistance Program for Survivors, a military service organization.

She's also been a widow and single mother since 2005, when her husband, Marine Corps Major John Ruocco, hanged himself in a hotel room near Camp Pendleton in California while awaiting redeployment to Iraq.

From the moment Kim and I met, we didn't just feel like fellow members of the suicide survivors community, we felt like soul sisters. Both of us had lost men we loved to suicide. Both of us are mothers, determined to do whatever it takes to help our children through the loss of their fathers. And both of us, being health professionals, still wonder what we missed and what we could have or should have done differently to keep men we were so close to from killing themselves.

Kim and John met in college, in a coed dorm at the University of Massachusetts in Amherst, and it was a classic case of love at first sight. John was a charismatic life-of-the-party guy, funny, thoughtful, larger than life, a loyal and dedicated friend who had a gift for making the people around him feel special. They were still deeply in love when they got married eight years later.

John had dreamed of being a Marine since he was a little boy. His Italian father and his Irish mother, both devout Catholics, wanted him to pursue something else, almost anything else, that would keep their son safe; and out of respect for them, John tried unsuccessfully to find a new dream. Kim assured him that she'd support whatever decision he made, and they were both very happy when finally, almost inevitably, John joined the Marine Corps.

He thrived, and he excelled, finishing at the top of every class, including flight school. He became a Cobra attack helicopter pilot, which he felt great about—the mission of the Cobra is to fly low over the ground troops in battle and protect them from threats, and he liked working closely with ground troops.

John's first duty station was in North Carolina. His and Kim's four years there set the course for the rest of their lives. Their two sons were born there. John deployed twice and was sent away for other training so that he was gone for months at a time. Two of three hurricanes that hit forced Kim and the babies to evacuate inland to stay safe. (She was a little chagrined to learn that when hurricanes are bearing down, Marine pilots race to move the aircraft to safety, while the wives and children are left behind.)

But by far the most devastating events of those four years were training accidents in which eight of John's friends were killed. John was on several of the missions where the accidents happened, and there never seemed to be time and space to grieve and recover—essentially, the drill was to attend the memorial service and then get right back in the cockpit for more training or deployment. Kim still remembers walking into the officers' club one night and seeing seven women made widows by those accidents sitting there, all of them in their twenties and thirties. "That would never be me," she thought. In other words, she says now, she was in total denial.

It was after those fatal accidents, and after the birth of their first son, that John went into his first major depression. He became anxious about flying, afraid he was going to make a mistake and cause someone to get hurt, or worse. During that depression John told Kim for the first time about a horrible event during his high school years—he'd had a head-on collision with another car, and the driver of the other car had died in the accident. He didn't get professional help after that tragedy, and the only advice his parents had to offer was, "Pray about it, and go to confession." So John went into the Marine Corps with a lot of unresolved grief and trauma that resurfaced with the loss of his friends.

Kim was torn. She had a lot of expertise on the subjects of mental health and depression, thanks to her degree in clinical social work, and she knew the importance of getting professional help. But she also knew that telling anyone outside their family that John was struggling might adversely affect his military career and jeopardize the wings he'd worked so hard to earn.

Instead, she focused a lot of time and attention on trying to help him, through exercise, a healthy diet, as low stress a life as possible, prayer, whatever she could think of to lessen his anxiety and pull him out of his depression. When he didn't seem to be improving, she finally convinced him to go to one of his superiors on the base and tell him what he was going through.

The superior's advice boiled down to, "Everyone goes through times like this. Take some time off, don't go to treatment, and don't take any medication—it might interfere with your ability to fly and keep your position." In other words, "Suck it up and don't tell anybody. You should be able to get through this on your own like everybody else."

When John did manage to shoulder through it and get to the other side of his depression, he apologized to Kim. "I'll never put you through that again," he promised her. "I was such a baby, such a wuss. I can't believe I did that to you and our son." He'd learned to view his anxiety and depression not as legitimate mental illnesses but as character flaws that wouldn't have happened if he'd been stronger and "more of a man."

John was given a prestigious assignment at the Pentagon, so he and Kim packed up their two sons and moved to Washington, DC. John's new duties put him in charge of placements and forced him to make a lot of decisions that were very unpopular and interfered with a lot of lives. As a natural-born people pleaser, he was struggling again, and the assignment was wearing on him dramatically.

Finally they started talking about leaving the Marines

and going home to Massachusetts, where both of their families lived, and where Kim had started a successful social work career at the renowned McLean Hospital when John had first joined the military. They came up with a plan in which he'd get out of active duty, join the reserves, and fly for commercial airlines. He'd still be doing what he loved, but with more stability; and they were hopeful and excited about their lives and their future when they would head home to their families, who would be waiting for them with open arms.

They were living in Oklahoma, where John was working toward getting flight hours to fly commercial in anticipation of moving back to Massachusetts, when the unspeakable terrorist attacks of 9/11 happened, an event that changed the trajectory of countless military families.

"This is going to change everything for us," John told Kim. "This will be war. They'll need me."

He'd promised his family he'd be moving to Massachusetts with them. He'd promised the Marines he'd be there if they needed him. He was training U.S. Air Force pilots in jets, and he was training to fly for Southwest Airlines in the hope of getting hired. Now he couldn't imagine leaving the U.S. Marine Corps because they would need him more than ever.

One day he said, "I'm tired."

Kim looks back today and still kicks herself for letting the cheerleader mentality of military spouses overshadow her better judgment and expertise. Instead of saying, "Of course you're tired! Let's figure out right now how to take some of this off your plate," she heard herself say, "You're John Ruocco! You can do this! You've got this!"

He decided that when the war started he'd get out of active duty and join a reserve helicopter squadron he knew would be deployed. The squadron was stationed in Pennsylvania, at least within striking distance of Massachusetts, where they'd just bought a house. It wasn't perfect, but it was the best they could come up with.

Before long, John's squadron was deployed to Fallujah, Iraq, for five months. It was a terrible, unstable period in Iraq; and in the short time he was there he flew seventy-five combat missions, flying at least once a day. By the time he got home for Thanksgiving in 2004, he was thin, withdrawn, agitated, and impatient, with no interest in eating his favorite holiday food and socializing with his family and friends. Kim did her best to make him comfortable and make it a traditionally happy Thanksgiving for their kids. She also tried to convince herself that it was unrealistic of her to expect him to be the same man he was when he left for a very difficult combat tour, and that it was understandable that he needed peace, quiet, and space. She was worried about him, afraid it was more than an adjustment problem, but she kept pushing those thoughts away and focusing on making sure he knew how happy they all were to have him home again for a holiday they always loved.

I instantly flashed back to how bad Rob looked and sounded in the days before he took his life. I'd decided it might be sadness about the divorce. In other words, just like Kim, I came up with the simplest, most obvious, and least frightening explanation I could think of.

John and Kim also had to deal with a couple of upsetting things that had happened while he was away: he didn't get the job with Southwest Airlines, and the squadron he'd attached to moved from Pennsylvania to San Diego, three thousand miles away from his family. They were scheduled to redeploy to Iraq in March, which required months and months of work-up training, so John was off to San Diego shortly after Thanksgiving, with not nearly enough time to reconnect and regroup before he was due to leave for his next combat tour.

John and Kim made a lot of cross-country phone calls in the weeks that followed, and the more they talked, the more apparent it became to Kim that John was really in trouble. She called him on Super Bowl Sunday, February 6, 2005, after she watched his beloved New England Patriots beat the Philadelphia Eagles. She expected to hear some excitement in his voice. Instead, he sounded terrible. He'd been in bed in his hotel room all day, and alarm bells went off for Kim when he admitted that he hadn't watched the Super Bowl—a game he loved and looked forward to every year.

"John, you've got to get help. It doesn't matter if you

lose your career, you've got to do this," she begged him. He not only agreed to go to a Marine counseling facility in San Diego called Behavioral Health; he also told her he'd scheduled a trip to Massachusetts in a few days.

"That's good," she thought, "he's making plans for the future." Then she took a deep breath and made herself ask, "Are you feeling so badly that you're thinking about suicide?"

Without a moment of hesitation he answered, "I could never do that to you and the boys."

I couldn't resist interrupting Kim to tell her about Rob's "absolutely not" reply when Dr. Simring asked him if he was having any thoughts of suicide. Kim told me that denial is actually a common response from people who are contemplating killing themselves, so she'd been as relieved to hear John's adamant "no" at the time as I was to hear Rob's.

Still, Kim knew that reaching out for help would be the hardest thing in the world for John to do. Operating purely on instinct, she got in her car, drove to Logan Airport, caught the red-eye, and flew to San Diego to support her husband and go with him to Behavioral Health.

She arrived the next morning and immediately called John. It gave her an ice-cold feeling in the pit of her stomach when he didn't answer his cell phone or the phone in his hotel room. She rented a car and started trying to track him down. He hadn't shown up for work. She called Behavioral Health and the emergency clinics on the base.

Nothing. No one had seen him. Her heart sank when she pulled into the parking lot of his hotel and found it filled with Marine Corps vehicles.

She jumped out of her car and rushed to John's room. She got to the door just in time to find a very upset Marine walking out.

She didn't even have to ask the question. She knew, and she fell to her knees. John was dead. He'd hanged himself. It was February 7, 2005, three months after he returned from Iraq.

And in those next several hours of shock and despair, without realizing it at the time, she was propelled into a whole new phase of her life.

As an unattended death, John's suicide had to be investigated. A team of policemen, detectives, trauma specialists, and a priest suddenly filled the taped-off hotel room. Kim was in a panic, laser-focused on the one thing on her mind: "How do I tell my boys?"

Her sons were extremely close to their dad. He was their sports coach, their playmate, their real live war hero, and they adored him.

"What do I tell them?" she pleaded to the Catholic priest.

"Well, you know what the Church thinks about suicide, don't you?" he asked.

"No," she said, "I don't."

He looked at her without a trace of compassion. "It's a mortal sin."

She was incredulous. "You want me to tell my kids that their father's dead and he's gone to hell? How dare you? How could you even say such a thing?" She completely lost it and started yelling, "Get out! Get away from me!"

The trauma specialist gently pulled her aside. "Mrs. Ruocco, your children are too young to understand suicide. You should just tell them their dad died in an accident."

Every instinct in her, and all her expertise, told her that was the wrong thing to do. But what good had her instincts and expertise done her when it came to saving John? She'd missed so much, all the signs that should have told her how much trouble he was in, all the signs that could have helped her save his life. She was too vulnerable and too much in shock to trust her instincts anymore; so she called her sister, who was taking care of the boys, and told her to tell them their daddy had died in an accident.

Kim flew back to Massachusetts that night, her mind reeling with grief and her brain exploding with anxiety as she tried to imagine how to navigate the path of this lie her sons had been told. How was she going to keep people from telling them the truth? How was she going to protect them from knowing there was no accident, their father had killed himself? They went to Mass every Sunday. How was she going to shield them from a Church that apparently believed their dad had gone to hell? How could she make sure everyone outside the family knew to stick with the accident story? Should she just lock her sons in the house with her and their family, keep them isolated for . . . how long? Days? Weeks? Months? That was impossible. But still . . . It made her angry to realize that protecting this lie was almost overshadowing protecting her two little boys.

Kim went through the next couple of weeks on automatic pilot, barely aware of all the traditional mourning activities going on around her and even less able to remember them. Her first crystal-clear memory of that awful time was a moment she'll remember for the rest of her life, a moment that snapped her back to sharp, total consciousness from then on.

She was driving the boys to her older son, Joey's, eleventh birthday party when he quietly confessed from the back seat, "You know, Mom, I think I killed Dad."

Struggling to keep herself calm, she pulled the car over and climbed into the back seat. "What do you mean, sweetheart?"

There were tears in his eyes from his broken heart as he finally unburdened his soul.

"The last time he was home we were eating nachos, and I asked him if I could salt his nachos. He said no, because too much salt is bad for your heart. But when he wasn't looking I salted them anyway. Dad must have had a heart attack, and that's why he had an accident."

As Kim described it, it "burned me to the ground." She knew intellectually that when something doesn't make sense to a child, they fill in the blanks to their detriment.

How had she not known that, of course, that rule applied to her children too? She wasn't about to let her son go on for one more minute blaming himself for something that was a lie to begin with—the only way for this family to heal, she realized, was through trust and honesty.

So, in simple, straightforward language they could understand, she told them. About their daddy's depression. About all the pain he was in. About how one day he was in so much pain he couldn't think about them, he couldn't think about her, he just wanted to make his pain go away. It wasn't their fault, not one bit of it; and from that day forward she would never make up stories again, she'd be completely honest with them, and she promised they were going to get through this together no matter what.

The military organization TAPS, Tragedy Assistance Program for Survivors, offers peer support and grief resources to families and loved ones of those who died while serving in our Armed Forces or as a result of that service, at no cost to the survivors. Kim turned to TAPS when she heard about their annual Memorial Day kids' camp weekend and adult healing seminar.

The kids had an amazing experience.

Each child at TAPS camp is matched one-on-one with an active-duty volunteer service member. There were six hundred children at camp that weekend. All but one of them were matched up immediately. The only one left was Kim's nine-year-old son, Billy, who was told, "The mentor you were originally matched with couldn't come, so we're trying to find you another one."

Billy was devastated, crying, feeling rejected, singled out of all those kids as the one no one wanted.

Then, within minutes, a Marine came up to him and asked, "Are you Billy?"

Billy, still crying, managed to nod.

The Marine knelt in front of him. "I have a story to tell you, and you're not going to believe it," he said. "I came back from Iraq and wanted to do something to give back. So I started Googling military kids and camps, and I found TAPS. I'm here on my own dime, by the way, and I took the training to be a mentor. I went into this room this morning and asked if any of the kids didn't have a mentor, and they said, 'Just Billy Ruocco.' Out of six hundred kids. I said, 'John Ruocco's kid?' And they said, 'Yeah.'"

Billy had stopped crying and was listening intently.

"Billy, I flew a lot of missions with your dad in Iraq. There were times when we came under fire, and your dad talked me back to the base. And now I'm here for you."

This wonderful Marine has been Billy's mentor and friend ever since, and it's been a great healing experience for Kim's sons and for the Marine—he's been able to tell them about their father's courage and leadership in combat, and they've been able to tell him about John as a dad. He came to their high school and college graduations and has been proud to be there for his battle buddy's sons, and

Kim and the boys can feel John's presence through him, as if John personally sent him to them.

Kim once had the pleasure of meeting Iris Bolton, a pioneer, author, and lecturer in the field of suicide loss, who told her, "There will be gifts in this. People don't like to hear that when they've first gone through the loss, but it's really true—if you're looking for them, if you're open to them, if you accept them, they'll be there."

I'd never thought of it that way; but when Kim told me that beautiful story, I realized that Alex, Chloe, and I were given an almost identical gift, when Rob's best friends said to my children, "You may have lost a dad, but you have three more of them right here." Yes, I absolutely believe John sent that Marine to his sons, and I absolutely believe Rob sent his best friends to my kids. The word *gift* is a perfect description.

As great an experience as Kim's boys had on that first weekend at TAPS, Kim's experience disappointed her. TAPS offered peer support for anyone grieving the death of someone who served in the military, no matter how that death occurred; because suicide is a whole other kind of death and grief, Kim found herself surrounded by people who were on a very different journey than she was. She was still wondering why and how John's suicide had happened; still wondering about the suicidal mind and how it works; still trying to figure out why she didn't see the red flags along the way; still trying to renavigate her faith after her Church told her that her husband, the finest man she'd ever known, a man who served his country with nothing but pride and passion and desperately needed help, had gone to hell for killing himself; still struggling with the shame and the guilt and the emphasis on how John died rather than how he lived and served, while other deaths in the military were honored with medals, monuments, and parades.

Kim felt so isolated and alone at that weekend seminar that she went to Bonnie Carroll, the president and founder of TAPS. Kim explained how much more complex the grieving process is for suicide survivors and why, and talked to her about suicide survivors' specific recovery needs. By then Kim had sought out other suicide survivors in the military and discovered that they were having the same struggles she and her sons were having, and she hoped that Bonnie and TAPS could find a way to help with their unique needs.

Without a moment of hesitation Bonnie said, "Let's build it." And with that, she and Kim started to build programs that address the challenges suicide survivors face, and they developed a three-part model that helps people evolve from brokenness to what she calls "post-traumatic growth."

Part one is stabilization, stabilizing suicide-specific issues and building a solid foundation for the grief journey. Among many other basics, it addresses common concerns like telling children what's happened in a developmentally appropriate way; navigating your spiritual beliefs, either within your faith community or on a new spiritual path; treating your own unresolved trauma and mental health issues; and identifying family problems that might get in the way of a healthy grief journey and helping to reframe those problems and heal them as the journey begins.

Part two is grief work, or integrating grief into your life. Loss and grief aren't a one-and-done event. They're a life-time process, a part of your life from the moment of the loss. Grief is love. You grieve because you loved. Grief work helps you move away from the trauma of how they died to remembering how they lived, and then helps you develop a new relationship with the deceased—the death of a loved one doesn't mean the death of the relationship, after all. So how do you continue that relationship in ways that are healthy for the survivor? Part two includes learning to re-late to the deceased and incorporate them into your life in a variety of ways, from traditions to communicating with them to embracing and celebrating your memories of them rather than pushing them away.

Part three is called post-traumatic growth. Once people have integrated their grief and their memories of the de-ceased into their lives, and created a new relationship with them, they find themselves wanting to make meaning out of their loss and find ways to honor their loved one. Some choose to do that by simply looking at the world with more compassion and appreciation. Others do it through creating a new purpose for themselves. Still others become peer mentors, serving as beacons of hope for those who are still in the grief phase of healing, or get actively involved in prevention work.

What Kim has found with the vast majority of suicide survivors she's worked with, and with herself and her boys, is a common thread of deepening empathy as the healing continues; a very kind, loving connection to the people around them; and an awareness of how what's happened to them measures up with what those other people are going through. That immediately took me back to a couple of conversations I had with my kids shortly after Rob killed himself.

When Chloe first returned to school, she talked to one of the members of Friends Helping Friends whose mother had died of skin cancer. When she was telling me about it, she said, "I can't imagine how horrendous it would be to watch a parent die this slow, painful death."

And Alex was driving me to his best friend's house for dinner one night when he said, "Mom, I never really thought about suicide, and how many horrible ways there are to kill yourself. But a lot of times people have to find the bodies, and they can never get that vision out of their minds. God, that must be so terrible."

My children had just lost their father, and they were already sympathizing with other people and realizing that, hard as it was to believe, those other people had it worse than they did. According to Kim, after all her years in the TAPS organization, it's a very typical survivor reaction and one that's inspired her and given her hope through her own healing process—that, and reigniting her spirituality.

She ended up pulling away from the Catholic Church because there was so much shame and guilt woven into the messaging. She's learned that the Catholic Church no longer believes that suicide is a sinful death, nor is it ever referred to as a sinful death in the Bible; but there are still a lot of old-school priests who preach against it. Whether or not that's their attempt at prevention, it's at the expense of the survivors and definitely contrary to Kim's belief in a loving, compassionate, forgiving God. She's finding a new faith community that believes in and celebrates *that* God, and her renewed spirituality is adding a whole new strength and joy to her life.

Kim's many years with the Suicide Prevention and Post-vention program for TAPS have led her to an enormous amount of research about the how and why of suicide. Of course, there's no simple answer, but she knows that the more she understands about it, the more she can contribute to its survivors, including herself and her sons. I shared something Dr. Simring said to me that's stuck with me ever since: "People will end their lives when they lose two things—hope for tomorrow, and a fear of death."

Kim completely agreed, with a few additions she learned

from reading studies by author and suicidologist Thomas Joiner, who's also a suicide survivor. People in any profession that almost requires a diminished fear of pain and a diminished fear of death, like the military or medicine, are already at an elevated risk of suicide. Add a loss of hope, and access to lethal means, or a specific "weapon" they can use to end their life, and it's heartbreaking but almost understandable that there are more than eleven thousand suicide survivor families in Kim's current TAPS database, all of them grieving the suicide of a military loved one, with three or four new ones reaching out every day.

And without a doubt one of the most powerful messages Kim had to share came from conversations she's had with people who've survived suicide attempts. All of us survivors who've spent countless hours agonizing over what we could have and should have done differently, the unanswerable "Why wasn't I enough?" questions, and "How could they have done this to me/our children/everyone who loved them?," can find some sad comfort in hearing that in every one of those conversations, those people described virtually the same thing: a perfect storm of stressors and emotional pain became so all-encompassing that they believed that perfect storm was going to be their forever state of mind. Their focus and their purpose narrowed to one thing, and *only* one thing: end the pain. They weren't thinking about their spouse, or their children, or their family, or their work, or the impact their suicide would have on everyone left behind. *End the pain.* In those final moments, that's all there was. That's all that existed.

It's heartbreaking to think of Rob, or Kim's husband, John, or anyone else on this planet being in that much pain, but so much for the haunting possibility that they just didn't care anymore. And even more of a reason to put an end to the stigma of mental illness once and for all and be proactive about mental health to keep people safe from being in that much pain in the first place.

Kim so beautifully articulated the concept that all this pain could actually lead to post-traumatic growth. Among the many other insights I got from her, she helped me understand why my kids and I, instead of letting Rob's suicide make us bitter and withdrawn, were starting to feel much more sensitive to life and the people in our lives, and more aware of the impact of our actions and our words and our behavior.

I still look back and marvel at what a difference the amazing suicide survivors I talked to made in my life and my healing, and what a personal loss it would have been for me if I hadn't reached out to them, especially with a couple of very rough milestones looming right around the corner.

CHAPTER SEVEN

Hanukkah, Christmas, and New Year's came and went uneventfully. Alex, Chloe, and I were together for the holidays, surrounded by family; and there were even fleeting moments when it didn't seem odd that Rob wasn't with us. But January 17, 2018, would be a different story—it was his birthday, after all.

With Rob's birthday approaching, we decided that instead of grieving and being sad, we'd celebrate and throw him a party, just the three of us, at our favorite neighborhood Italian restaurant. We waited at the bar for our table, texting back and forth with friends of Rob's who wanted us to know they were thinking about us; and I ordered a glass of Prosecco for our toast to the man without whom Alex and Chloe wouldn't even exist. I'd just taken a sip when Chloe urgently reminded me, "Mom, you're doing a dry month!"

Years earlier Rob had started declaring every September a dry, alcohol-free month, as an exercise in will power. It inspired me to kick off 2018 with "Dry January," announce it on *Good Morning America*, and invite viewers to take the "Dry January Challenge" with me. With the exception of during my two pregnancies, when I abstained from alcohol completely, I've always been, at most, a moderate drinker. My motto is "Two and through." But I was curious to see if I could follow the same advice I give my patients every day, to reduce their risk of breast cancer by either giving up alcohol completely or at least diminishing the amount of alcohol they consume. "Physician, heal thyself," so Dry January it was, until January 17; and let me go on record as saying that one absent-minded sip of Prosecco, to toast Rob's birthday, was my only slipup.

Rob's birthday also gave me a reminder that none of us has any business assuming there will always be a "next time." His birthday the year before happened to come along six days prior to our divorce being finalized. Amicable as it was in general, we'd had an argument about who knows what. I was mad at him, and to drive that point home, I deliberately didn't call or text to wish him a happy birthday. I felt justified but kind of badly about it at the time. Looking back on it after dinner with Alex and Chloe that night, I deeply regretted it, with Rob not around to apologize to anymore. It's a lesson learned the hard way that I hope I won't forget—no unfinished business. It hurts to live with it later.

Rob's birthday was on Wednesday. On Saturday I got a call from his friend Art in Florida, who'd been kind enough to adopt our Labs, Nigel and Remy, after Rob's suicide. Remy, the yellow Lab, had developed cancer during the year; and Art and his wife, Elizabeth, had done an amazing job of giving her all the medications and treatments she needed to fight it. But she was losing the battle, she was miserable and in pain; and while Art was feeling strongly that it was time to let her go, he wasn't about to make that decision without checking with the kids and me.

Heartbreaking as it was and always is, I completely agreed, and I knew Alex and Chloe would too—holding on to an animal in pain with no hope of recovery, especially an elderly animal like fourteen-year-old Remy, is nothing short of selfish and cruel. It was very emotional for both me and Art, and I thanked him and Elizabeth from the bottom of my heart for taking such amazing care of those dogs since the day they arrived in Florida.

It wasn't until I hung up the phone that it hit me, and I still believe it to this day, because I don't believe in coincidences: Remy held on until Rob's birthday. Then she just wanted to go Home and be with him, her beloved alpha male, playmate, and best friend. I love picturing that reunion.

IN MANY WAYS, ROB'S BIRTHDAY WAS AN EMOTIONAL PRECURSOR to the milestone I'd been dreading most—February 11, 2018, the one-year anniversary of the day Rob took his life. It seemed impossible that a whole year had passed. I could remember every detail, right down to every sight and smell, of every second of every minute of that day when I let myself go there; and I was grateful that I had a busy day ahead to keep my mind from obsessing over it. I was flying back from a business trip, arriving early that morning. My mom was picking me up at the airport, and we were driving up to Connecticut for one of Chloe's travel hockey games. Then she'd drive Chloe and me back to our apartment, where Alex would join us for a quiet family evening, not being maudlin, just being together and making sure none of the three of us was alone on that of all nights.

Of course, the hockey game was in one of the countless rinks on the Eastern seaboard that Rob had been in thousands of times, but I pushed that potential trigger out of my mind. This day was going to be tough enough without dragging extra baggage into it, and Mom and I were there to focus on Chloe, not Rob. Chloe played well, I'm honestly not sure whether her team won or lost, and then she and Mom and I headed to Mom's car for the trip home to Manhattan.

There were two problems. One was that it was pouring rain. The other was that the back seat of Mom's car was outfitted with two baby seats for her grandchildren, Evan and Tanya's little boys. It had been fine on the way to Connecticut, with just me and Mom in the car. But now it was me, Mom, and Chloe, none of whom could fit into one of those baby seats.

As everyone knows who's familiar with baby seats, the

manufacturers' assumption seems to be that all of us have a PhD in engineering, which is exactly what it takes to install those things and remove them. The three of us took turns trying to dislodge one of the seats, butts hanging out the car door getting drenched in the rain. There were days when we would have found it hilarious. This was not one of those days.

Finally, out of sheer frustration and a complete lack of success, Mom threw up her hands and announced that Chloe and I could have the front seats, with me driving; and she would just smoosh herself in the back between the baby seats for the two-hour trip back to Manhattan. Chloe and I might have gone along with that idea if it weren't for the obvious downside that this would leave Mom without a seat belt, which was out of the question. She was so tired of the whole thing that she didn't care. We did. She'd be fine, she said. We were sure that's what her daughter-in-law, Tanya's father, thought, we said, exactly three years ago today, when he was killed in a car accident, not wearing a seat belt.

The whole thing escalated into a ridiculous, completely uncharacteristic argument, with all three of us chiming in at the top of our lungs. Mom defiantly wedged herself between the car seats, Chloe and I climbed into the front seats, and as I pulled out of the parking lot Mom ended some diatribe with, "It just makes me want to kill myself!"

Chloe promptly burst into tears. I promptly yelled back,

"How could you possibly say something like that today of all days?"

My mom is a retired pediatric nurse. She's a kind, nurturing, empathetic woman, and she and Chloe are very, very close. She was as shocked as we were at what had just come out of her mouth.

We rode at least an hour in total silence before we slowly thawed and started working our way back to each other. Mom felt awful. We all felt awful. And incredibly, even though it couldn't have been more obvious, it took us a while to figure out that none of what happened had anything to do with baby seats or seat belts or being angry at each other—we'd all been reacting to the heightened stress and emotion of an anniversary we were still trying to process. But we got through it, and in the end, we were just happy to have that day behind us.

I'll probably always wonder if there's something a little dark, or jinxed, or energetically bizarre about February 11.

It will never be just another day for Alex, Chloe, and me.

It will never be just another day for my sister-in-law.

And it will never be just another day for a woman with whom I have more in common than she or I ever imagined when we first connected.

"Jessie West" is a celebrity. She's about to start writing her memoir, so rather than run the risk of upstaging her story in any way, I'll use an alias for her. For the record, I'll be first in line to buy that memoir.

It's not just our age and our children that we have in common—we're only seven months apart, and we both have sons in their early twenties. She also lost her ex-husband (I'll call him "Mark") to suicide, an ex-husband she didn't think of as an "ex" at all, an ex-husband she still loved, who still loved her and was still very much a part of her life. How many people understand that losing an ex to suicide can be as utterly devastating as losing a spouse? And how many people am I likely to meet whose grieving process is on exactly the same timeline as mine—because her ex-husband took his life on February 11, 2017, the exact same day Rob did?

Jessie met Mark six years after her first marriage ended, and they had their first date on her forty-second birthday. They were deeply in love from the very beginning. He was funny and charismatic and tender, a quiet, very spiritual man with a heart that was all about helping people.

Mark had been diagnosed with bipolar disorder many years earlier, a fact he revealed to Jessie right up front. By his own admission, he struggled with self-esteem issues and a lot of demons because of it, and he'd experienced psychotic episodes in the past. She wasn't dissuaded in the least. She "got" him, she loved him, and her soul was committed to him from their first night together. She didn't just know she wanted him in her life, she knew that somehow he was essential to her; and she felt like the luckiest woman on earth when they got married in 2012.

It was an idyllic marriage for the first couple of years. They never argued or even raised their voices to each other, and he was a wonderful stepfather. He expanded the scope of her already deep spirituality and this world's relationship with the spiritual world, introducing her to concepts that were new and thrilling to her, like the power of the number 11.

Spiritually, the number 11 represents twin flames, a sacred union between eternal soulmates who've been fortunate enough to find each other on this earth. Eleven became "their" number, a powerful sign between the two of them that they were meant to be together, always, no matter what. Mark even had the number 11 tattooed on his neck.

Jessie had never experienced depression in her life, or been exposed to it, so she didn't know how to interpret Mark's chronic migraines and periods in which he'd have to force himself to get out of bed and be excited about anything. But then, in September of 2014, she saw a change in him. He seemed happier and more motivated than he'd been in a while; and she was encouraged, until his sudden enthusiasm escalated into a horrifying full-blown manic episode that included abandoning his car by the side of the road because he didn't need it anymore—he could time-travel, and he could fly.

Needless to say, it was a nightmare. Mark was evaluated as having a mental disorder that could potentially make him a danger to himself or to others and was involuntarily detained for a 72-hour psychiatric hospitalization; and Jessie felt she had no choice but to follow her therapist's advice and file for divorce a month later. He went from the hospital to a treatment facility. He didn't want to be there, he didn't want to be medicated, and he was only going through the motions to appease Jessie, so it wasn't effective.

Through all that, Jessie and Mark never stopped loving each other; and in 2015, even though their divorce had been finalized, he came back to live with her. No one around her wanted her to let that happen. And she couldn't deny that she'd been in nonstop fight-or-flight mode, sleeping with one eye open, since that terrifying manic episode. But he was fragile. He needed her. She knew the exquisite heart and soul of her Twin Flame that were trapped inside his mental illness, and she wanted to free him, and save him.

Jessie did everything she could possibly do for him from the moment he moved back in, searching for the right plant-based meds he believed in, making sure he ate in the hope he'd regain the thirty pounds he'd lost since his manic phase began, going with him to therapy appointments, and keeping their home and their lives as stable, peaceful, and stress-free as she could. Her sons, who loved Mark too, were incredibly brave and supportive; and Jessie made sure to let them be teenagers and leave the adult responsibilities for Mark's healing to her. It was exhausting, and she could never let herself relax, but not once did she have second thoughts about having him there.

Sadly, in the end, all her best efforts couldn't prevent the inevitable. In October of 2016 Mark had a second, very dramatic, very scary manic episode that resulted in the police being called to detain him. He was immediately hospitalized on a psychiatric hold again. Mark's mother and sister tried to get help for him, while Jessie stepped back and resigned herself to the fact that she and Mark would always be together spiritually, but he was suffering and out of control, and it wasn't healthy for her and her sons to be with him physically anymore.

On January 29, 2017, Jessie received a text from him that read, "I can't live without you." She texted back, "Yes, you can, and you're not without me, but I will never be a caretaker for anyone ever again." His reply was a simple, "I hear you loud and clear."

She found out later that on that same day, after that conversation, he went online and bought a gun.

On February 9, Jessie was leaving for a commitment in London. The day before, she got another text from him that ended, "I cherish every moment. Good night, I love you, angel."

On February 11, 2017, just after Jessie had completed her commitment, she got a phone call from Mark's sister. He'd disappeared, after e-mailing his sister a suicide note. Everyone else thought he was missing. Jessie knew instantly that he wasn't missing. He was gone.

He was found two days later, in his car. He'd killed himself with the online gun while Jessie was thousands of miles away and there was no chance of her being the one to find him.

Of course, the emotional pain was excruciating for many months—as she put it to me when we talked, she was hurting so deeply because she loved him so deeply, and "you can't have the ecstasy without the agony." For the first time in her life she experienced a depression of her own, not wanting to get out of bed, not wanting to take a shower and pull herself together, not wanting to see or talk to anyone, cocooned in her stunned grief and plagued by the inevitable what-ifs of a suicide survivor.

She knew how troubled he was, and that his suicide wasn't her fault. She also knew that if she'd taken him back she could have kept him alive . . . but only until the next time. . . .

She knew he wasn't meant to be here as long as she wanted him to be, and she felt the full force of the trauma of losing the one thing, other than her children, she'd been yearning for all her life, her soulmate, her Twin Flame, her guide through a rich, beautiful world of spirituality that was deeper and more profound than any other belief system she'd ever known.

And it was that world that brought her the most healing after Mark's suicide. It was almost as if he'd made sure she'd have their eternal connection to comfort her when he left this earth and sent her to someone who could help reassure her of that connection. After trying pretty much every traditional grief resource available and receiving little or no relief, Jessie found herself turning to a highly reputable psychic medium.

If you've ever been to a psychic, and/or a psychic medium who can communicate between the spirit world and our world, you know that many of them speak in such generalities that what they're "communicating" could apply to almost anyone. Jessie went in fully prepared for that possibility and came away absolutely certain that this woman had connected with Mark and that he was speaking through her. The medium was so impossibly specific that weeks of research couldn't have unearthed the information Mark passed along to Jessie through her. Any doubt that Jessie might have had that Mark was still with her, healed, at peace, and waiting for her on the Other Side, vanished in that one transformative hour. It was clear, thanks to his messages to her, that while his illness had prevented him from having power here in the physical world, he'd regained his power now that his spirit was free from his body.

She began to notice the Twin Flames number 11 all around her.

Of course, it was on February 11 when he took his life.

She held a memorial service for him on the beach where

they first met, and when she offered Mark's ashes into the ocean, eleven birds flew overhead.

She spoke about Mark's mental illness and suicide at a charity event in Florida a little over a year after he took his life. She noticed the time as she stepped up to the microphone. It was 1:11 P.M. She spoke for twenty minutes without a single glance at her notes—she literally felt as if she was just the vessel and Mark was speaking through her.

She produced a legacy film on a subject he felt passionately about. It had its world premiere on March 11, at 11:00 A.M.

Even my first phone conversation with her happened to start at 6:11 P.M.

She and I agree that we're not interested in trying to convince anyone of these signs that Rob and Mark are still around us. We know, and that's good enough for us. In Rob's case, it wasn't just my finding him sitting on the edge of my bed on the third night after his death. There was another incident I'll never forget that took my breath away.

The heart-symbol connection between Rob and Chloe was between the two of them, very sweet and having nothing to do with me. In fact, I didn't know a thing about it until later, and neither did our friend Laura.

Laura had known Rob since college, and she was married to one of his best friends, one of Alex and Chloe's three "dads." So one day she opened her kitchen cupboard to find a coffee mug with hearts all over it sitting on the shelf in front of her. She hadn't bought it. In fact, she'd never seen it before.

Within an hour she was at my apartment, looking completely mystified as she handed the mug to me.

"What's this?" I asked her.

"It's for Chloe," she said. "Rob sent it."

She had no idea how or why she knew that, or how she knew she was supposed to bring it to me. She was even more blown away when I let her in on the special significance heart symbols held for Chloe and her dad.

I gave the mug to Chloe and told her the story. She's had several "unexplainable" spiritual experiences in her life, and there wasn't a doubt in her mind that her father had sent it to her through one of his closest friends.

There isn't a doubt in mine either.

Those reminders from our deceased loved ones that they're always around us, very close by, are incredibly reassuring; but they can't take the place of having them physically here with us, or put a magical end to our grieving. And the same was true with Jessie. More than a year after Mark killed himself, she came down with sciatica, a painful condition affecting the sciatic nerve that extends from the lower back down the back of each leg. She couldn't move for six weeks, and she became convinced that the grief she'd been trying to repress had been storing itself in her nervous system.

Rather than turn to traditional medicine for help, she followed what she knew would have been Mark's strong preference and began treating herself with the controversial protocol of the late Dr. John Sarno, who believed that physical pain is often the brain's way of providing protection from deep emotional issues. His strategy for addressing that pain includes a lot of journaling and writing essays on everything from anger, trauma, sadness, and guilt to self-imposed pressure from certain personality traits to anything that's causing stress in your life.

The Sarno protocol worked for her. The back pain lifted in about six weeks, and she noticed that a lot of her grief and heaviness lifted along with it.

I can't think of a more beautiful testimony to her years with Mark than Jessie stated to me toward the end of our conversation about him: "If I knew it was going to end exactly the same way, I would sign up again tomorrow because of everything I've come away with."

They wrote their own vows for their wedding. His simply read, "I vow to continue loving you." That promise is now tattooed on her arm, in his handwriting; and she doesn't doubt it for a minute. She knows he's at peace, he's healed, he's with her, he's waiting for her, and he'll never stop loving her. Now that the anguish of losing him has subsided and she can think and feel clearly again, she still feels what she felt the day they got married—like the luckiest woman on earth for having loved and been loved by him.

What especially resonated with me as I listened to Jessie's story was how, divorced or not, she treasures the gift of having known Mark. I feel exactly the same way about having known Rob, because he gave me my children, and he was an amazing father to them for eighteen years. There's no more precious gift he could have given me and them, and it's a gift that couldn't have come from anyone else but him. Jessie's positive memories of Mark bring her a lot of comfort, much like the comfort I get from watching Alex and Chloe and thinking of how proud Rob always was and, I insist on believing, still is of the people they are and the people they're becoming. It's because of them that I realized I could look back on Rob's and my story and echo Jessie's sentiments exactly: If I knew it was going to end exactly the same way, I would sign up again tomorrow because of everything I've come away with.

CHAPTER EIGHT

THE LAST HOME ICE HOCKEY GAME OF THE SEASON EVERY year at Lawrenceville is Senior Day. It's a very big deal, and very emotional. For some of the graduating senior players it's the end of their high school hockey career. For others it's the end of their competitive hockey career. Before the game each player is called onto the ice, one by one, to pose for pictures with their parents, who present them with bouquets of flowers; and there's a huge banquet in their honor after the game.

Chloe was a junior in 2018. Mothers of the junior players are each given an assignment for this special day. Mine was to make framed photos of the senior players, which I was happy to do. I arrived at the rink, dropped off my assignment, and then made my way to the upstairs tier of bleachers to watch the pregame ceremony. Each senior stepped into the spotlight on the ice. A mom and dad, beaming with pride, took their place on either side of their daughter, gave her flowers, and made her feel like a queen, while flashbulbs lit up all around them like fireflies. It was beautiful, and I burst into tears.

My poor Chloe. How was she going to get through

this next year without Rob? He was the world's proudest hockey dad. I could still see the delight on his face when we first put her on ice skates at three years old, and when she started playing hockey at the age of five. For the first five or six years, until she was old enough to do it herself, he would tie her skate laces for her, because they had to be tied really tightly; I never could get the hang of doing it right myself. He of all people should be there with flowers to have his picture taken with her on Senior Day. Where was she supposed to get the strength to smile for all those cameras, knowing that her dad wasn't right there by her side, and knowing why?

And where would I get the strength to see her through one of the most special days of her hockey career, her solo parent when there should have been two of us? Alex would be proud and happy to bring flowers for his sister and pose for pictures with us. My parents would come, and Evan, and Rob's best friends, just like they'd be there for her other once-in-a-lifetime senior events, like graduation, and getting accepted to college. They all loved her, and they'd all be so happy for her. And there would be no way around the fact that they'd also be stand-ins. They wouldn't be Rob. They wouldn't be the father who belonged there. They wouldn't be the father who made the choice not to be there, who made the choice to miss every major event in the rest of his children's lives, and to leave the rest of us with the impossible task of trying to make up the difference.

It made me unbearably sad. But more than that, it made me angry, with nowhere to put it. There were days when, no matter how hard I tried, I couldn't push aside my anger toward Rob on Alex and Chloe's behalf and replace it with something more loving, more positive, and more grateful. This was one of those days.

While I'm sure it's not true for everyone in our situation, anger was never the overriding emotion for me or my kids after Rob's suicide. I think in our case it was a matter of not wanting to start down that road because we might not be able to stop if we let ourselves go there, and turning into bitter, angry-at-the-world people wasn't a future that appealed to any of us. I certainly wasn't about to let the only parent my children had left be an angry mother, that's for sure. In fact, it was the "only parent my children had left" reality that was my biggest trigger when it came to anger, that awareness that when I was feeling tired, or overwhelmed with work, or sick, and Alex or Chloe needed something, I could no longer say, "I'm sorry, I can't. Call your father." That made me very angry, for myself and for my kids. In general, though, anger wasn't my default toward Rob at that point, I just wasn't sure why. At least not quite yet.

I'll never look back on my conflicting anger issues about

Rob's death without thinking of a conversation I had with Melissa Rivers. She was only a year older than Chloe when her father, Edgar Rosenberg, killed himself. Even years after his suicide, she told me, she'd go to friends' weddings and have to excuse herself when the father-daughter dance was announced, because it was too painful a reminder that she didn't have a father to dance with anymore. I hated knowing that Alex and Chloe had countless situations like that to look forward to in their lives; but as Melissa pointed out, while the pain never completely goes away, "you learn to go through moments that suck" and keep reminding yourself that time really does heal.

I was always a huge fan of Melissa's mother, Joan Rivers. I thought she was hilarious, of course; but I also admired how strong and fearless she was, conquering the old boys' club of stand-up comedy and late-night television at a time when everything in the business seemed to be stacked against her.

I ran into Joan Rivers one day at CBS, where one of the talk shows had just surprised her with a birthday cake. She was well into her seventies, impeccably dressed, with her usual perfect hair, makeup, and posture, and as we passed each other, I admit it, I couldn't resist approaching her and introducing myself.

"I just have to tell you, it's such an honor to meet you," I said. "You're a true legend."

She gave me a little self-deprecating eye roll and shot

back, "I'm so damned old, and there were so many candles on that cake, I'm surprised I didn't burn down the whole set. What I really am is a true fire hazard."

I found Joan and Melissa nothing short of amazing on *Fashion Police*. It was no surprise that they were funny, sharp-witted, and right-between-the-eyes honest. What fascinated me was their obvious, incredible ability to recover from a suicide in their family and actually excel as they went on with their lives. I couldn't imagine how they did it.

Then it happened to me, and I had to find out the hard way.

Joan Rivers's husband, Melissa's father, Edgar Rosenberg, was in Philadelphia, wrapping up a few days of meetings. He called Joan and told her he was flying back to Los Angeles the next day. Instead, the next morning, August 14, 1987, he swallowed a fatal overdose of Valium and killed himself at the age of sixty-two. He was found by his business partner, Tom Pileggi, on the bedroom floor of his hotel suite. Before taking his life, he recorded three cassette tapes—one for his business partner, one for Joan, and one for Melissa, to eliminate any suspicion of foul play and to say good-bye. He explained that his depression and his declining health after a massive heart attack three years earlier made him feel like a burden to the people he loved, and he couldn't go on.

Naturally, it was a complete sucker punch to Melissa's mind, heart, and soul. She remembers that when the numb shock began to wear off, she deified her father and blamed her mother because, she said, after all, "When you're in free-floating anger, you've got to blame somebody." Her parents' marriage was terrible at the time of her father's suicide; so blaming her mother came easily, while her mother blamed her father and never really forgave him. In fact, after Edgar took his life, Melissa stopped speaking to Joan. It took therapy and about two years for them to reconcile.

She credits two people with getting her through those first awful months. One was an amazing grief counselor, who walked her through what to expect mentally and emotionally in the aftermath of a loved one's suicide. "You must, must, *must* go to a mental health/grief professional," she told me. "Trust me, your girlfriends have no idea how to handle this." It made me smile. It's so simple and so obvious, but I'd never heard it put better.

The other person who made a huge difference in Melissa's life while she was still reeling from that indescribable trauma was actress Mariette Hartley, whose work Melissa knew from any number of television series and movies. Melissa had never met Mariette Hartley. To the best of her knowledge, neither had her parents. But out of nowhere, Mariette reached out to her, not as a professional on the subject of suicide survival but as someone who'd been there herself.

Mariette Hartley, it turned out, was twenty-two years old when she lost her father to suicide. He was an artist, a successful ad agency executive, an alcoholic, and a manic-depressive; and one horrible day in 1962 he shot himself in the head in the family's Brentwood, California, apartment while Mariette and her mother were in the next room.

It made an indelible impact on Melissa that this total stranger was generous and compassionate enough to pick up the phone and call her when news of Edgar Rosenberg's suicide hit the papers. Thirty years later she still tells Mariette, "You saved my life." To have a friend to talk to who knew and had lived through the shame, the guilt, the blame, the feeling of sticking out like a sore thumb, and all those other monstrous emotions made a huge difference in her healing.

Mariette let her know that all the crazy emotions she'd be going through were okay, perfectly normal, and, hard as it was for her to believe, temporary. It would take years, but sooner or later they'd even out—she wouldn't be feeling this way for the rest of her life.

"Anger? Absolutely. A nonstop stream of what-ifs and if-onlys? Count on it, but don't let them take over your mind, because they lead nowhere except around and around in a pointless circle, and you'll drive yourself insane. Feeling isolated because of society's misguided stigma against suicide? Of course you will. For a while. Just remember, the stigma comes from fear and ignorance of why suicides happen in the first place. You did nothing wrong, and you have nothing to apologize for."

From the very beginning, Melissa was well aware of the stigma, she just wasn't having it. People would approach her, without a clue what to say or do, and offer a sad, "I'm so sorry your father died." To which she would snap back, "No, he didn't die, he fucking killed himself!" It was all she could do not to add, "This happened! Don't pretend it was something else! Why are you making me feel like I should be embarrassed?"

Joan, in the meantime, prided herself on being strong; and in public she never allowed her husband's well-publicized suicide to make her appear weaker or more vulnerable. "If you're having a tough time," she'd say, "go home and have a weekend wallow, then get up and start moving your life forward." But in private, in reality, his suicide leveled her in every way; and because of the anger and blame between her and Melissa, they couldn't be there for each other. Melissa did let her mother convince her to go back to the University of Pennsylvania when the fall semester started, even though it was the last thing she wanted to do. "Your life is not stopping. You need routine. You need normal," Joan told her. Looking back, Melissa agrees that her mother was very right and very smart about that.

Several family friends had immediately become like father figures for Melissa, which helped a lot; and when she returned to campus, five of her closest guy friends protectively circled the wagons around her and, as she put it, "drug her through school, and her grief, kicking and screaming." (Decades later, they're still like brothers to her, by the way, which means the world to a woman with no siblings.) For the most part, though, she was painfully aware that everyone around her, from classmates to professors, had read the headline news that her father, Joan Rivers's husband, had killed himself weeks earlier. She experienced that same scarlet letter sensation I did after Rob's suicide, that hollow, aching feeling of being whispered about and judged and making people uncomfortable just by walking into a room.

The first year after the suicide, she remembers, was a nightmare. The second year was harder. For the first year she had her guard up, braced for every holiday and birthday, knowing they were going to be horrible, and they were. Her life felt unfamiliar, like she was living in some weird netherworld where everything looked the same but nothing felt the same, and nothing made sense.

Toward the end of the first year she experienced a turning point in her recovery. She was at summer school, having an especially hard night, sitting on a bench with a friend. As a light rain started to fall her friend asked, "Did you respect all your father's decisions in life? Because you need to respect his decision in death. You might not like it, but you need to respect it."

Melissa took a moment to think about it, then replied, "I *don't* like his decision, just like I didn't like his decision when he grounded me, or took away my car keys. But you're right, I had to respect those decisions, so I guess I have to respect this one."

That blew me away. Chloe had said exactly the same thing to me, around a year after Rob's suicide. "It was Dad's decision to take his life, and we have to respect that." I was amazed at her maturity at such a young age, and I was amazed at Melissa's.

It was in the second year that Melissa's guard dropped; and she woke up to discover that, no, it wasn't a nightmare, it was all harshly, undeniably, cruelly real, the new irrevocable normal. It was also in that second year that she began to notice occasional glimmers of happiness, and the tremendous guilt that went with them. "Okay, I can feel my face smiling," she thought, or, "I hear myself laughing, I must be having fun, but that can't be right, when I feel so totally empty inside."

Little by little, though, as the anesthesia of grief wore off, the actual feelings started coming back, instead of just the motions of those feelings. From time to time she'd realize, "Hey, I had a pretty good day," and make it a goal to string together a pretty good day or two in a row. She would never have chosen this new normal, but no one ever gave her a chance to vote. It was what it was, fair or not fair, so at the very least it might as well be bearable.

Another huge part of Melissa's healing was getting involved with a grief support center called Our House—not just going to meetings but also becoming a speaker and activist. She came to believe that if you're a suicide survivor, you're almost obligated to reach out and help others who are going through the same thing, exactly as Mariette Hartley had reached out to her to let her know that she wasn't alone, she wasn't losing her mind after all, and she really would get through this.

From the first moment she stepped through the doors of Our House, Melissa learned how blind this very different kind of tragedy really is. Suicide doesn't discriminate. It even reaches into families who think it could never happen to them, which makes the shame, and the stigma against it, even more preposterous. And no matter how widespread the group of survivors, ethnically, economically, culturally, or religiously, this one irrefutable fact of their lives brings them all together and makes them all alike.

She sends that message from the very beginning when she speaks, with the simple, straightforward greeting, "Welcome to a shitty club that nobody wants to be in. We live in a society in which everyone wants to be special. Well, guess what—this is the one time in your life when it's amazing to be normal, to not be special, a time when you can look around and say, 'Everybody around me has gone through this.' Because every emotion you're having or will have, we've all had, or will have. The last thing you want to hear right now is, 'They're in a better place,' right? Me too! You want to shout back, 'Well, they may be in a better place, but *I'm not!*' You're also wondering, 'What if I'd made that one more phone call?' or 'What if I'd been nicer the last time we talked?' 'Why wasn't I enough?' I'm here to tell you the truth, and it's just a fact, take it from me—*you were enough!* The suicide you're mourning was *not your fault.* And here's another fact you can count on—you're going to be okay."

She means it. She knows it. She lived it. She's also accepted that, inevitably, the pain will creep up on her from time to time for the rest of her life. It's not about expecting the pain to go away forever, it's about knowing that when it hits, it's normal, she understands where it comes from, and after what she's already been through, she can count on being strong enough to deal with it.

She's also well aware that she'll always love her father with all her heart; and just like when he was alive, that love isn't negated one bit by those moments when she's furious with him. "You chose not to be here for my graduation, or to walk me down the aisle at my wedding, or to meet your grandson? Fuck you!" As time and healing have gone on and her relationship with him has evolved, she's learned to forgive herself for those moments, because she's learned to forgive him.

Melissa's relationship with her mother obviously evolved too. She felt very vulnerable as an adult about having only one parent, and she and Joan reconciled and became even closer than they were before Edgar's suicide. For almost thirty years it was just the two of them, two survivors who fiercely loved and knew each other and never had to explain a thing.

And then, on September 4, 2014, Joan Rivers died at the age of eighty-one, after undergoing what was supposed to be a routine endoscopy at Yorkville Endoscopy in Manhattan. Melissa later won a settlement against the clinic for performing unauthorized medical procedures on her mother. I remember reading about the case and, as a doctor, being stunned at what looked to me like an egregious case of malpractice—including a selfie taken by one of Joan's doctors with Joan, under anesthesia, visible in the shot.

Melissa's mother was suddenly, wrongly, gone too, "ripped away in the blink of an eye," as Melissa put it. Understandably, much of the trauma of her father's suicide came rushing back to her and sent her spinning. Now she had no parents, no siblings, no one to share a lifetime of memories with, and she had to do battle with that dark, hollow feeling of "I'm all alone."

What kept her going was the son she adores, to whom she unapologetically announced after her mother's death, "You're it, buddy. I'm going to be overprotective, and you're going to have to deal with it." Her son and his grandmother were extremely close; and when Joan died he said to Melissa, in tears, "Nothing will ever be good again." She instantly flashed back to feeling exactly the same way after her dad's suicide, and she held him and promised, "Yes, it will. It will just be different," a promise she knew she could keep after years of healing.

In fact, she's convinced that what she went through with her father has made her a better parent. His suicide and the grief counseling and survivors' work it led to have created a vigilant, empathetic mom with her eyes wide open and a painfully well-informed awareness of the increasing number of teen suicides. While suicide doesn't run in the family, she knows that mental health issues and depression can; and she's diligent about watching her son's social media accounts and his moods and, if he's down, getting him to talk about it. And she frequently reminds him that no matter what happens or how bad things might look, suicide is not an option. "Nothing in this world is worth it—no girl, no grade, no game, no insult, *nothing*."

She also admits, with a laugh, to being vigilant when it comes to her boyfriend. He calls it controlling. She calls it being at her saturation point on suddenly losing people she loves. He took a trip recently. She insisted on constant updates every step of the way. Finally, exasperated, he reminded her, "Airplanes don't just fall out of the sky, Melissa."

"In my life they do," she replied.

He couldn't argue.

Melissa continues to be very active in her passionate work with suicide survivors, both privately and through Our House. In fact, in 2013 she received the Good Grief Award for the openness, honesty, and respect with which she addresses her father's suicide and the subjects of death and grieving. As she and I were ending our conversation she said, "Jen, if your kids ever need to talk, give them my number, or give me their numbers and I'll call them."

It literally brought tears to my eyes. A lot of people are great at talking the talk. With that one invitation she made it clear, and very personal, that she also walks the walk.

Of course, being Melissa Rivers, she made sure I was smiling by the time we hung up. She had written *The Book of Joan: Tales of Mirth, Mischief, and Manipulation* after her mother died, and she quoted the dedication to me: "To my mother, who I miss every day, and to my father, who, starting this past September, is no longer resting in peace."

I took away some very valuable insights from talking to Melissa, especially since she was my kids' age when her father killed himself. I'd been so scared on my children's behalf that the major milestones in their lives would all be ruined; but there she was, having lived it, saying that sure, some parts of those milestones weren't great—in fact, some of them "sucked." But her relationship with her father continued to evolve, even though he was gone, and as it evolved, those milestones became easier to deal with as she figured out what to expect and learned more and more practical survival skills. Her matter-of-fact approach to her reality—i.e., "Welcome to a shitty club that no one wants to be in"—reminded me so much of Alex and Chloe and helped normalize for me what they're experiencing.

Hearing her story was like peering into the future and seeing my kids thirty years down the road, with marriages and children of their own—how resilient Melissa was and is, how resilient Alex and Chloe are and will be, and how this tragedy will make them better, more informed, more aware parents, just as Melissa's tragedy did for her. Particularly as a parent, I hung up from that conversation feeling more reassured and almost encouraged about the rich, full lives my kids can look forward to.

CHAPTER NINE

I T WAS EARLY SPRING OF 2018, THE BEGINNING OF THE SECOND year after Rob's suicide. Melissa Rivers warned that the second year was harder than the first. Oh, God. It was tough to imagine that was even possible.

Work-wise, I was busier than I'd ever been in my life, both in my private practice and at ABC. When I'd occasionally pause to take a breath I'd find myself thinking, "Am I really busier, or is it just that I feel busier because of what I've been through?" Ultimately, my answers to those questions were yes and yes. I definitely was objectively busier, but I felt too that because of Rob's death I was more determined about getting it all done. It was a blessing to be busy.

I was also finding that when I'd be with very close friends talking about Rob's suicide, I could go from being totally fine to starting to cry in a split second. That's when I'd wonder if I was burying too many of my raw emotions beneath the surface of my busyness. Was I really healing, or just tricking myself into believing I was by literally not allowing myself time to think about it? There were times when I felt proud of where the kids and I were, performing at a high level at work and in school. There were other times when I wondered if maybe we were doing *too* well. Is that a problem? And another horrible thought kept creeping in: I'd never been a woman who second-guessed herself. Now it seemed I was almost preoccupied with it. Was this ever going to stop? Was it just another part of a new normal I had to get used to? Or maybe it was another facet of the second year being harder than the first, which I'd also been warned about by an amazing woman named Carla Fine.

IN 1999 CARLA'S BOOK *NO TIME TO SAY GOODBYE: SURVIVING THE Suicide of a Loved One* was published. Sadly, it was autobiographical. The loved one in the subtitle was Dr. Harry Reiss, her husband of twenty-one years and a board-certified urologist in her hometown of New York City.

She and I obviously had a lot in common, and I was excited to get to know her. This may sound like an odd word to use to describe a conversation between two women who've lost their doctor husbands to suicide, but in addition to being insightful, articulate, wide open, and nononsense honest, I found her to be an absolute delight. It's no surprise that she's a renowned author, activist, and speaker for suicide survivors' groups and professional organizations all over the world.

Carla Fine and Harry Reiss met and married in college. She was on her way to a Master of Science degree, with honors, from the Columbia University Graduate School of Journalism, and a very successful writing career. He was on his way to a medical practice at St. Vincent's, Cabrini, Bellevue, and New York University hospitals, with a private practice in Manhattan.

Harry's parents, Viennese Jews who left Austria for South America in 1938, lived in his native country of Colombia. In 1988, his mother passed away. His father died a year later, sending Harry into a deep sorrow. Carla tried to talk to him about it and suggested he get help. He blew it off.

"I'm sad, Carla. I've lost both my parents," he pointed out. "This is a normal reaction to double grief. I can get through it. If I were dancing around the house singing, maybe *then* I'd let you convince me to see someone."

On December 16, 1989, four months after his father's funeral, Harry was very late coming home from the new office he and Carla had just bought in Chelsea. Carla started calling, but there was no answer. Finally, after several more unanswered calls, she got concerned enough to go to the office and check on him.

She found him fully dressed, lying on an examining table, still hooked up to a self-administered IV carrying a mixture of thiopental and heparin into his veins. He was dead at the age of forty-three. There was no note.

Carla looks back on that moment as dividing her world into a frozen "before" that would never exist again and a shocking, instantaneous, nonnegotiable "after." And her first reaction was a stunned, frightened, furious, "Are you kidding me?!"

"It was like when a couple who'd been married as long as we were had an argument," she told me. "You yell, he yells, he storms out the door and slams it behind him; then, eventually, the door opens again, he comes back in, and you figure it out. But this time it was like he had the last word and stormed out, but that door would never be opening again. And married couples discuss things. 'I'm thinking of buying a new car,' or 'I'm thinking of taking up tennis.' No 'I'm thinking of ending my life'?! I don't get any say in this?"

Of course, along with that rage came an instant flood of other emotions—confusion, fear, guilt, blame, too many to even identify. But somehow she was still thinking clearly enough to grab the phone and dial 9-1-1.

The police and the ME were there within minutes. The police were struggling with the idea that a physician would kill himself; and in the sudden organized chaos, a detective from the 10th Precinct stepped up to Carla and asked if she was a nurse and if she knew how to give an IV.

She screamed back, "You think I killed him? Are you crazy?"

What Carla knew about suicide at the time was that, according to the news, it was some rare, tragic thing that happened to troubled celebrities. It wasn't even on her radar in the real world, least of all her world. So it was a surprise to her that suicides had to be investigated by the medical examiner's office in New York. Following an autopsy and investigation, it was clear that Harry had methodically planned this—he'd ordered the lethal drug about a month earlier and administered it to himself.

Carla still remembers the spectacle in front of her husband's office building when she finally stepped outside— cop cars and emergency vehicles everywhere, law enforcement personnel and paramedics streaming in and out of the entrance doors, while people walking their dogs, checking their mail, heading home with groceries, just going about their normal lives, curiously gathered to see what all the excitement was about. The most devastating, intensely personal moment of Carla's life had become street theater.

The first couple of months were a blur. Carla didn't have the option of falling apart. She and Harry had no children, but Harry had patients in the hospital, patients scheduled for surgery, patients scheduled for consultations and examinations, and she felt responsible for finding other doctors to take over for them. She was also trying to deal with a reaction from those around her that completely blindsided her. There seemed to be a whole lot of blame being aimed at her, looks and implied questions from friends and from Harry's colleagues and patients, questions like, "What did you do wrong to make him so unhappy?" and, "You must have seen signs that this was coming, why didn't you stop him?" Those unspoken questions stung, especially since they were the same questions she was asking herself. Suicide, she quickly discovered, was a different kind of death. Shameful. Attracting judgment like a magnet. All about the why while the survivors stood shattered and isolated in the background.

Of course, that same *why* haunted Carla. She kept examining moments, events, and passing conversations in her marriage to Harry like a detective. She'd replay them over and over in her mind like a movie she kept rewinding, desperate to solve the mystery of what pushed this man she loved, whom she knew better than anyone else on earth, over such a fatal, final, methodically planned edge. "If I'd stepped in here. . . ." "If I'd said something else there. . . ." "What about that time I snapped at him . . . ?" "Did he really mean to die alone like that, or was he hoping I'd walk in earlier and stop him . . . ?" The medical examiner told her Harry would have been asleep within seconds of pushing that IV into his vein, and dead within minutes. He gave himself ten times the lethal amount of thiopental. He meant this. She became consumed with those last moments when he walked in the room to that examining table and lay down. He must have known she'd be the one to find him. It enraged her, and broke her heart. He inflicted that horrifying image on her for the rest of her life. How dare he do that to her, his wife, his partner, his lover, his best friend? How dare he? But still, to choose to die, and to die alone . . . her Harry . . . he must have been so tortured.

It was shocking to her that the people around her seemed to be going out of their way not to mention Harry at all, probably for fear the dreaded *suicide* word might come up. She already felt abandoned enough, by him. Now, in addition to feeling profoundly sad, guilty, blamed, and shattered, she felt like a pariah, isolated in general, almost punished for something he'd done.

And then there was the fear and pressure of being left with a pile of financial problems. Harry had been the primary breadwinner of the household. They'd just mortgaged their co-op to buy his office in Chelsea six months earlier; and because Harry had such a bright future, they'd been given a double mortgage that was now her responsibility. Carla had a book contract when he died. But now she found her ability to write had been paralyzed, if not extinguished, and writing was the only way she knew to support herself.

She was drowning, financially and emotionally, and she needed somewhere to turn. She joined Safe Place, a grief support group run by the Samaritans of New York.

It saved her life.

She found herself surrounded by a room full of compassionate people who were freely using the word *suicide* instead of avoiding it as if it were the most obscene slur in the

English language. She found people who'd been tortured by the same unanswerable questions, isolation, and stigmas she had, and were ready and willing to talk about them. She found new friends who could say, "I know exactly how you feel," and mean it. And she found a new purpose—to let other suicide survivors know that they weren't alone, and that there's hope ahead if they're open to it and make it their business to look for it.

It took months, but she was finally able to put words on paper again. She started looking in bookstores and found nothing about surviving the suicide of a loved one; and she said to herself, "If there's no book about this out there, then it's up to me to write it." The result was her wise, comforting, heartfelt *No Time to Say Goodbye: Surviving the Suicide of a Loved One.*

She started being asked to speak to groups throughout the country about surviving suicide, and discovered that the more open she was with the survivors she talked to, the more she had to teach them, and the more she learned. She put together a powerful collection of messages, not platitudes, that she still shares with suicide survivors all over the world.

The first year, she says, you're in a total state of anesthetized shock.

It gets harder before it gets easier, and the second year is harder than the first. The numbness is wearing off, most of the busyness is over with, and you find yourself thinking,

"Okay, I did everything right last year, I did everything I was supposed to, and they're still dead! No fair!" It really starts to sink in that this is permanent, and nothing you can say or do is going to change it.

Around the third year, the haze starts to clear a little, especially when you look back and realize that first you dealt with the suicide, then you dealt with the death. And by the fourth or fifth year, you start to believe that maybe you can move on after all. The loss will always be part of you. It will only define you, and the one you lost, if you let it. Your grief can sentence you to the dark, bitter life of a victim, or it can fuel a rich life of finding ways to honor your loved one and keep them alive through you. The choice is yours.

In the meantime, there are a few practical ways to start with that may help.

- Protect your health.
- Seek out other survivors.
- Surround yourself with people who make you feel comfortable.
- Get professional help if needed.
- Accept that you and the world around you have changed.

As Carla pointed out to me, and she's exactly right, there's no magic switch to turn off your inevitable fixation with the final hours of your deceased loved one's life before they chose to end it. She learned to look at it this way: when someone dies of cancer, or a heart attack, or in a car accident, we don't obsess over their last minutes, when they were struggling for every breath and moaning in pain. We don't reduce their lives to nothing more than that one narrow, final time frame. We owe the same respect to suicide victims that we owe to everyone else we've loved and lost—a determined focus not on how they died but on how they *lived*.

She also brought up something I'd never thought of before, easier said than done, but I promised I'd try. There's no easy way, she said, to sweep your mind clear of the inevitable guilt cycle of what-ifs and if-onlys, the barrage of "what did I do/say, or not do/say, that made this happen?" But it's very much worth the effort to start replacing those self-defeating thoughts with lighter, more productive ones. Whether we were aware of it or not, there were undoubtedly many, many times when we did or said the *right* thing and saved our loved one from killing themselves, when we loved them off that ledge without even knowing it. If we're going to fill our heads with questions that will never be answered, why not insist on filling them with ones that remind us how often we just might have been heroes?

And in the end, it's essential to remember that, unlike children, whose suicides tend to be much more impulsive, adults are very deliberate about it. They know what they're doing, and it's what they choose to do. None of us chooses it for them. We survivors choose to live. "I'm sorry Harry did this," Carla told me, "but I'm not going down with him."

In fact, not only did she not go down with him, but she and her life started opening up in ways she never imagined. She found that she and the suicide survivors she spoke to and heard from when they read her work went from being strangers to friends in no time. They had an immediate close connection, regardless of race, religion, politics, income, status, occupation, background—mental illness and suicide are equal opportunity stigmas, after all. She got to know a whole new world of strong, amazing, resilient people she would never have had the pleasure of meeting otherwise; and in the process she discovered that she was becoming a stronger, more compassionate, more empathetic and complex woman than she ever imagined she could be. Even now, thirty years after her suicide survivor journey started, she keeps finding deeper layers to herself. She's a better person, a better writer . . . and a better partner.

Carla was three or four years into healing when she started dating. She and a few of her girlfriends from Safe Place had more than one good laugh imagining going to a singles bar, being asked to dance by some random guy, and responding, "Hi. I'm Carla. My late husband stuck an IV in his arm and killed himself. Thank you, I'd love to dance." Not likely to result in a second dance.

She did end up meeting and falling in love with a wonderful man named Allen Oster. Early in their relationship she told him exactly what had happened to her husband. He never asked why, or even implied that maybe she was to blame somehow. He was just sorry she'd been through such a tragedy and promised to be there for her when she needed to talk about it and when she didn't. He wanted to look forward, not back; and when he proposed, she didn't hesitate to say yes.

She had to admit to her therapist, though, that she was afraid she might run screaming out of the wedding. She'd been down that aisle before. She was deeply in love with Allen. She'd also been deeply in love with Harry, and look how that turned out. She'd always prided herself in being perceptive; but she hadn't spotted so much as a hint of mental illness in Harry, or a single red flag that he might be planning to take his life. If her instincts had failed her so miserably when it came to Harry, how could she trust them when it came to Allen? She couldn't invest her heart like that again and end up going through the same devastation she'd barely managed to survive for the past four years.

On the other hand, when she focused on her life with Harry instead of how it ended, she felt nothing but gratitude. She was happy being married to him. She began to see it as a testament to her happy memories of him that she still had the capacity to love, and love deeply, and be excited to embrace this opportunity to be that happy again with Allen.

Carla and Allen have been married for over twenty years now. She continues to be a prolific author, international speaker, and guest on a wide variety of television and radio shows, committed to embracing suicide survivors, exactly as Safe Place embraced her when she was feeling so alone. Her life is rich and purposeful, not in spite of her tragic, painful journey but because of it.

My second year was under way, and I was discovering that yes, it really is even harder than the first.

Believe me, I've never lost sight of how lucky I am. I have two full-time careers I love. I have two kids I adore and enjoy spending time with, and they actually seem to enjoy spending time with me too. Living in the city made it even easier to hang out with Alex, and I wasn't about to let anything stand between me and Chloe's hockey games.

In fact, one night we found ourselves wondering if Rob was as determined to be there as I was.

It was late March 2018. The final game of the Atlantic district play-offs, a do-or-die must-win if Chloe's travel team was going to qualify for the national championships. The heart-stopping game ended in a tie; and I almost reached for my phone to text Rob that we were going into overtime, followed by ten or twelve exclamation points. But there was enough excitement in the air and enough music blaring through the rink's loudspeakers to snap me right back to reality. I never took my eyes off Chloe and the look of pure joy on her face as she and the rest of her team gathered around their coach for a last-minute strategy huddle.

After a brief, breathless wait, the players took the ice again. Overtime started, and in what seemed like no time at all, we won! We were headed to the national championships! Oh, my God! The crowd went crazy, and so did I. It took me a few long minutes that seemed like forever to get through the celebrating fans, parents, photographers, and players and reach the bench to wrap my arms around my thrilled, heroic daughter.

"Congratulations!" I yelled into her ear. "I'm so proud of you!"

"Thanks, Mom, but I knew we were going to win!" she beamed back.

I asked how she could possibly have known that.

"Because Dad's here!"

It sounded much more specific than a typical "with us in spirit" comment, and I stared at her. "What are you talking about?"

"Didn't you hear the song that came on before overtime started?"

"Not really, no, I wasn't paying attention," I told her. "Why? What was it?"

" 'Werewolves of London'! That was Dad!"

I was clueless. I remembered the song, vaguely, but,

"What does 'Werewolves of London' have to do with your dad?"

"He and I used to listen to that song on the way to hockey games!"

Now, write that off as a coincidence if you want. I just find it impossible to believe that, with literally millions of random songs that could have come on between regulation play and overtime, "Werewolves of London," a hit in the 1970s that Rob and Chloe loved listening to together forty years later on their way to hockey games, "just happened" to be the song that led Chloe's team to a major victory. As far as I'm concerned, that "coincidence" is even more unlikely than the idea of Rob sending that song that night to let his daughter know he was there, cheering her on.

By all appearances, between my kids, my patients, and my TV commitments, I was busy as usual, which came with its own downsides as winter turned to spring of the second year. Inevitably, all those people who went out of their way to be supportive and attentive in the first year saw me fully functioning again, assumed enough time had passed that I was back to normal, and went back to living their own lives. As they should have, no doubt about it. But I noticed the quiet. I noticed the absence of people calling or coming by "just to check on you." I noticed that people stopped even mentioning Rob, for my comfort level and theirs, I'm sure. It wasn't that I missed the special attention, it was that everyone seemed to be acting as if Rob had never existed, let alone that he'd leveled us by killing himself. I didn't want people dwelling on it, it just felt as if it mattered too much to be old news already.

Another downside was that, while it had been a blessing to be so busy in the first year, in the second year it started to drain me. One of my "shivah girlfriends" who'd lost her husband to suicide had warned me, "Don't be surprised if you can't get as much done as you used to," and she was so right. All my life, when I'd finished my commitments for the day and still had time to spare, I'd think, "Great, I can take care of these two or three other things before I go to bed." Now I'd think, "I could, I just don't feel like it," and shut down. It was a big change for me, and a hard one—it felt weak and undisciplined and lazy, and I expected a lot more of myself than weak and undisciplined and lazy. It took a while, but with Dr. Simring's help I learned to be patient with myself, give myself permission to say, "It's okay, you don't have to, you can take care of that tomorrow," and recognize that "weak and undisciplined and lazy" was really nothing more and nothing less than "This is a Rob's death thing." They say that the first step in solving a problem is identifying it. It's true. Learning to identify a "Rob's death thing" when it came along at least allowed me to be a little easier on myself.

I was also learning the hard way to expect to be blindsided every once in a while and accept that a) it will hurt, and b) I've been through worse, and I'll get through it.

Chloe and I were at our local bank one Saturday afternoon, our family bank for decades, when we ran into one of my favorite people. He was one of the Ob-Gyns who trained me when I was a resident, a kind, caring South American man and a great surgeon whom I hadn't seen since the end of my residency fourteen years earlier. We greeted each other warmly, and I loved introducing him to my tall, beautiful eighteen-year-old daughter who'd been six months old when I started my residency.

We were doing the usual catch-up chatter, those rapid-fire "How've you been?"/"Where are you now?"/"Whatever happened to [fill in name of mutual acquaintance from that era]?" questions when he suddenly tossed in, "How's your husband?"

Or he could have just reached down and yanked the rug out from under me. I'm sure my face turned as pale as Chloe's did, while a nearby teller we'd been doing business with forever said to him, in Spanish, "Don't you know?"

It was an awful moment. If it had been someone who didn't mean anything to me, I might have escaped with a simple "He passed away" or something. But this was an old friend. For the first time I said, out loud, "Rob's gone. He took his own life." Chloe and I told him what happened, very briefly but honestly, and it was stunning how numb and surreal it felt as we were saying it that Chloe and I had lived through it.

Needless to say, my friend was absolutely mortified; and needless to say, I felt so sorry for him—all he'd done was ask the most innocent, well-intentioned question, and it wasn't his fault that he hadn't heard about Rob. Chloe and I assured him that there was nothing to apologize for, he and I hugged good-bye, and we all went on with our day.

Sure enough, it hurt. A lot. Like any sucker punch will, intentional or not.

Sure enough, I got through it.

And getting through it was the best I could do, because underneath all the busyness and "normal" I made sure to present to everyone around me, I was hiding the fact that, inside, there were many times when I still felt completely shattered.

CHAPTER TEN

I WAS ABLE TO RELY ON REQUISITE PIECES OF MYSELF TO COME through on cue for my viewers, my patients, my staff, and my family and friends. Sometimes I felt as if I'd managed to put all those pieces back together again. Other times, though, I still struggled to rediscover that strong, confident, accomplished, has-it-all-together woman I'd been for almost fifty years.

Dr. Simring and I talked about it a lot. She kept telling me that this "one step forward, two steps back" feeling was normal in the second year as the fog lifts and reality sets in. I'd get through it, I just needed to be patient. In the meantime, "Remember the goals and the priorities and the energy of the person you were before the suicide happened, and give that 'you' the respect of keeping those things going however you can."

I trusted her, and she was certainly thinking more clearly than I was. So I took her word for it and followed her advice as best I could, including recommitting myself to my obsession with the best physical and mental therapy the me I used to be had ever found—exercise. The woman I was functioned much better when she worked out regularly than when she didn't. Maybe that would help me find my way back.

No matter how tempted I was to blow it off sometimes, or how many excuses I thought of to do it tomorrow instead, I kept appointments with my trainer at the top of my priority list. And I even managed to head back to Soul-Cycle. Yes, the place where I was busy pedaling away while Rob was jumping off the George Washington Bridge. I'd finally learned to drive across that bridge without falling apart. Surely I could learn to overcome my fear that something horrible might happen if I let myself start spin classes at SoulCycle again.

I did. It felt great, I became addicted to it again, and everyone I loved lived right through it.

It was at the beginning of class one weekend when the instructor, James J., gave me a public shout-out, something casual and lighthearted like, "And there's Dr. Ashton, one of our star members, with her perfect attendance record." As the room darkened for class to start, I happened to glance to my left and saw a young girl two bikes away from me, who mouthed the words, "Are you Dr. Ashton?" I nodded, and she added, "I know Chloe."

At that moment class got under way, preventing me from pursuing the conversation. And when class was over we all went our separate ways, so I didn't get a chance to properly introduce myself. But I did happen to mention to Chloe that someone she knew was in my spin class.

"I know," she replied. "She told me she saw you there. She's one of my suicide survivor friends at Lawrenceville. Her father killed himself when she was only thirteen."

Thirteen. Oh, my God, that poor girl, she was just a baby. I had to hear her story.

"Rebecca Butler" (not her real name, at her request) had a wonderful childhood. She and her three siblings, two of them older, one younger, were very close; and her parents weren't just husband and wife, they were also best friends who never disrespected or even raised their voices to each other.

After many successful years on Wall Street, Rebecca's father moved the family to her mother's small hometown in the Pacific Northwest, where he started several prosperous businesses. Rebecca was a daddy's girl from the day she was born. She even looked like him, while her siblings looked like their mom, and it was a great source of pride to her that she and her father were so close.

She doesn't remember anything out of the ordinary leading up to it, but she does remember the evening when he came home from work and told his wife, "There's something wrong with me. I'm not thinking clearly. I need help."

Her father had suffered concussions during his childhood that hadn't really been treated properly or resolved, and he was sure that those concussions were at the core of several mental problems he wanted so much to finally put behind him. Rebecca's mom immediately took action and found him a therapist, who began treating him and put him on medications.

One month to the day after he announced that he needed help, he drove to a quiet park and shot himself. His wife and their two older children were the ones who found him.

Rebecca was thirteen. Her childhood died the day he did.

She remembers being overwhelmed with grief, pain, anger, confusion, and shame. She couldn't begin to comprehend what had happened, let alone process it; and she could hardly turn to her friends for support—they were thirteen too, with their childhoods still intact. In fact, they were suddenly uncomfortable around her and seemed to be avoiding her as much as possible. She hasn't forgotten her first day of high school. One of the teachers was taking attendance and called out her name, and a girl across the room in a class of twenty-five students yelled, "Oh, you're the girl whose dad killed himself!"

Rebecca and her large family embraced her and one another and became closer than ever. Her mom, who'd just lost not only her husband and the father of her four children but her best friend as well, was amazing. She seemed to put her own grief aside, was always there for them, and saw to it that they got into therapy right away. Rebecca saw three different therapists before she found one she connected with. "It can take a while to find the right fit," she said.

That's so true, and so remarkable for such a young girl to understand it and keep looking. I know some adults who've needed therapy but rejected it altogether based on a wrong fit or two. Rebecca knew at thirteen that she needed help to sort out everything that was going on inside her, from agonizing grief to feeling like an outcast at school to the worst loss she could ever have imagined, the loss of the father she adored, who'd always made her feel like the most special person in the world.

After about a year she became resistant to therapy and stopped going, for a couple of reasons. For one thing, she came to resent the monotony of showing up once a week "to go into a room and cry for an hour." For another, looking back, she realizes that she was letting anger become her default, her comfort zone, almost a habit, while her therapist kept trying to get her to explore other areas of her grief that hurt too much. Anger is the safest emotion, after all. We get hurt less when we're angry than when we're open and vulnerable. She felt guilty if she went even a day without intensely feeling something, and anger was the most readily accessible. A constant loop of questions kept plaguing her—"Why didn't you love me enough to stay?" "How could you leave me when you knew how much I loved you?" "Why wasn't I enough?" And when those questions started to make her sad, she'd actually force herself to re-place that sadness with anger instead, because it was the one emotion she knew she could handle.

Rebecca blew me away when she summarized that part of her healing process by saying, "Let yourself get angry, but don't get addicted to it. It can become a scary comfort to feel that pain."

A "scary comfort." I'd never heard that description of anger before, let alone from someone so young.

When she was finally ready to face those other aspects of grief she hadn't processed yet, she sought out therapy again; and looking back, she deeply appreciates the growth that's come from it. For the first couple of years she'd delib-erately tried to block out her memories of her dad, because they made her too painfully aware of the fact that he was gone, by his own choice. But thanks to time and a lot of work with her therapist, she started to find joy in remem-bering what a wonderful man he was, what a wonderful father, and what a wonderful husband and best friend he was to her mother throughout their twenty-year marriage.

"I can't let his last act on this earth define his life," she finally decided; and four years later she's found that rather than weighing her down, her memories of him are propel-ling her forward. She's stopped expecting the pain to ever go away completely. Instead, she's made peace with letting it coexist with all the many other elements of her busy, productive, happy life.

Her Christian faith also brings her great comfort, as she understands that this tender, loving man who was in such confusion and despair in his last moments on earth is at peace on the Other Side, now and forever. She's sure she would never have survived the loss of her father without her own deeply personal relationship with Jesus. And there's a bit of irony that hasn't escaped her: "Sometimes the stigma of being religious is almost as bad as the stigma of suicide—say 'I love the Lord' to some people and they can't get away from you fast enough, as if it might be contagious." Then again, she also understands why there's a saying that goes, "I love Jesus, it's Christians I can't stand."

She believes that everyone is entitled to their own way of getting in touch with their higher power, by whatever name they call it, and wonders about many Christians, "Whatever happened to 'Judge not, lest ye be judged' (Matthew 7:1)?" She just wishes for every other suicide survivor a faith that gives them the certainty she's found through Christianity, that this life isn't all there is, that our loved ones are happy and whole and with us whether we can see them or not, and that we'll be with them again someday in God's arms.

Today this remarkable young woman considers herself blessed, not by having lost her father but by having had him as her dad to begin with. Her large family has grown even larger, with a stepfather and a stepbrother she loves very much and an older brother, a senior in high school when their father took his life, she describes as the most amazing person she knows.

She's excelling at Lawrenceville, looking forward to college, and moving ahead with pride rather than sorrow that she was and always will be a "daddy's girl."

"Everything in life happens for a reason," she says. "Our lives are full of stories, actions and reactions, and intricate patterns. We may not know the reasons for them now, but we will someday."

I'D SPENT A LOT OF TIME THINKING ABOUT THIS WHOLE ANGER issue. It seemed to come so quickly and naturally for most of the suicide survivors I'd talked to, including Rebecca. I'm half Italian, and a Taurus. Anger isn't exactly a foreign concept to me, although I usually abandon it as a waste of time. And no doubt about it, I'd had spasms of anger toward Rob after he took his life. But for the most part, I felt much more sadness than anger when it came to him, and I kept wondering why.

I figured it out during a big project I felt compelled to start in April—it was time to clean out Rob's storage unit, which I'd been paying for every month since he died. Anyone who's been through the after-death cleanup knows that it's an exhausting, sometimes emotional, sometimes incomprehensible chore. Boxes of clothes? Sure, okay, I get that. College yearbooks? No problem. Countless pots and pans from a man who treasured cookware the way some people treasure fine art? Nice additions to the "donate" pile. But a deflated soccer ball from Alex and Chloe's childhood? Really? The more hours I spent going through Rob's belongings, the more the word *stuff* took on a whole new meaning.

Mom met me there once or twice. The kids met me there a few times. They found several things of their dad's they wanted to keep, and I enjoyed watching them get excited about hanging on to tangible connections to him. It was also touching to discover that he'd saved some mementos from our marriage—most of all, an inscribed book of poetry he'd given me when we were still newlyweds, still in love. I kept those mementos, gladly.

The real logistical nightmare was the result of what a voracious reader Rob was, and he was most definitely *not* a Kindle person. He liked *books*—holding them, arranging them on shelves, physically browsing through pages, and collecting them. I'm not exaggerating when I say there must have been sixty or seventy boxes of books piled in that storage unit. The question was, what the hell was I going to do with them? The kids didn't have room for them, and neither did I, even if I'd wanted them.

Chloe came up with a brilliant idea. She and Alex went through the books and set aside the ones they knew were his favorites. Then, rather than hang on to the books themselves, which they'd never get around to reading, she took the dust jackets to make a giant framed collage, protected by art glass, that she and her brother can enjoy for the rest of their lives. I loved that and wished I'd thought of it.

Most of the time, though, it was just me, a few hours a week, going piece by piece, book by book, through every item Rob had deemed worth keeping to the very end of his life. And as I sorted those hundreds of books, I answered my own questions about my lack of post-suicide anger toward him.

It was in the last years of our marriage, long before we turned to marriage counseling, that Rob made his unforgettable, unapologetic proclamation, "All I need to be happy are my books and my dogs." I'd worked through the profound sense of failure and abandonment I felt when, as far as I was concerned, he'd withdrawn from me in favor of being alone, in his favorite chair, head down, engrossed in the pages of whatever nonfiction story he'd apparently decided was far more interesting than I was.

What I admitted to myself while I was sorting through those endless boxes of books, aka the "other woman" in Rob's life, was that I'd also worked through my profound anger toward him back then, due to my perception that he'd essentially turned his back on me, our marriage, and our commitment to each other. I wasn't about to try to compete for his attention, or forbid a grown man from reading in his own home, and he certainly had no patience with discussing a problem that, as far as he was concerned, was my problem, not his. So I went on about my business, and I fumed, in kind of a perpetual state of "all pissed off and nowhere to go," until finally I realized that being angry with him was hurting me much more than it was hurting him. It was counterproductive, it fixed nothing; and eventually it just burned out until, except for occasional circumstantial spasms of it, I had no anger left for Rob anymore by the time he took his life.

There was a certain peace in coming to that realization while I kept slogging through all those books and boxes of the rest of Rob's stuff. It took forever. Sometimes the cold reality would hit me—"Oh, my God, look what I'm doing. He's really gone!"—and I was almost reluctant to finish, because that would be "the end." Sometimes I just wanted it over with, so I could finally move on from this awful grief.

And, I hoped, from the vivid, upsetting dreams that had started interrupting my sleep.

Except for the first few weeks after Rob's suicide, I've been an amazing sleeper all my life. I've always been able to fall asleep in seconds, almost as if it's one of my jobs, and sleep soundly until my alarm goes off. I've never even had any use for a snooze button. If I had dreams, which I assume I did, they were apparently pleasant and unmemorable enough for me to sleep right through them.

But suddenly, a year and three months or so into my recovery, what I'm sure was a lot of unresolved trauma began acting itself out in the form of nightmares and waking me up at least one night a week; and most of those nightmares involved—ready?—water. Not the beautiful, welcoming water I've spent as much time in as possible since I was a baby, to the point where I'm almost more comfortable in water than I am on dry land. No, the water in these dreams was violent, frightening, and overwhelming. I'd find myself on a beach, for example, and see a massive tsunami wave bearing down on me. Or I'd be in the middle of a hurricane, in blinding rain, trying to make my way through the rushing water of flooded streets.

I don't think you have to be Sigmund Freud to figure out the emotional symbolism of "killer water" to a woman whose ex-husband killed himself by jumping off a bridge. These nightmares were exhausting and upsetting, and I had no idea how to make them stop. I was afraid, and still am sometimes, that they'd keep recurring for the rest of my life. Just when I'd think I was really through the worst of the pain and getting better, another tsunami dream would frighten me out of a sound sleep in the middle of the night and I'd think, "Who am I kidding? I'm really not getting better at all."

I'd never questioned my feelings before. Now I seemed to be questioning them a lot, which made me even more anxious to move on. I just had no idea to what.

The last thing on this earth I expected was falling in love.

It's an understatement to say that dating was the farthest thing from my mind, not just after Rob's death but long before that. Even when our marriage ended and he started dating, I wasn't interested. I hadn't dated since my mid-twenties, when I first met Rob. Now, at the age of forty-nine, it wasn't even on my radar. I had two high-powered careers, I was financially independent, my kids were eighteen and nineteen, my life was already full and busy enough, and I was dealing with plenty of my own healing and recovery issues. I didn't need a man to deal with on top of all that, and I certainly wasn't about to go into a relationship in which I'd be the emotionally needy one, or the one who needed to be taken care of.

I was also convinced that I was probably too much for any man anyway—too self-reliant, too unequivocal about my kids coming first, too career-driven, too overloaded with my own emotional baggage to have patience for anyone else's, too been there/done that. The only man who could possibly interest me would have to be smart, professionally accomplished, thoughtful, ethical, honest, financially secure, playful, romantic, and fully prepared to sweep me off my feet. Oh, and gorgeous and sexy wouldn't hurt. In other words, a man I was convinced didn't exist.

I was wrong.

It was late spring of 2018 when a mutual friend introduced us. His name was, and is, Todd. I trusted the mutual friend enough to know that he wouldn't have introduced me to a deadbeat, or a loser, or a man with the personality of a flounder, and this man seemed very bright and very attractive. On the downside, he was also a doctor—exactly last on my list of someone I wanted to be set up with. Our friend obviously thought this would give us a whole lot in common. And of course it did. But let's just say the words *refreshing change of pace* didn't leap to mind.

I decided not to be so quick to judge, though, and from that very first night on, Todd was amazing. I had already figured out, with Dr. Simring's encouragement, that I owed it to myself, and to him, to drop the "perfect" façade and be completely transparent from the very beginning about everything—Rob's suicide, what it did to my kids and me, how shattered I still was, and how tentative I was about trying to reconstruct myself, with a long way left to go. It was like breaking a lot of my oldest, most hardwired habits in the get-acquainted phase and learning a whole new set of communication skills with no edit button, the "This is who I am, take it or leave it" approach, fully prepared for him to choose "leave it." Instead, he was gentle and he was compassionate and powerful enough that it didn't scare him off one bit. In fact, by the end of the evening it was obvious to both of us that there wasn't just a date in our future, we were starting a relationship.

Once that became a reality and I was sure he was going to be significant in my life, it was important to me to tell Alex and Chloe about him. They insisted on meeting him, of course, and he was eager to meet them too. I wasn't a bit surprised that they all liked one another. Todd approached them like a new friend rather than a potential new stepfather; and he was gracious enough, in the process of talking about what great kids they are, to compliment me *and Rob* on how well raised they obviously were. Not once did he question all the family photos and pictures of Rob in my apartment, or disrespect him in any way. And as I vacillated between having the world's longest fuse and the world's shortest, and between feeling like the strongest woman on the planet because of what I'd been through and the weakest and most fragile because the wounds were still so new, he was steady as a rock, with the patience of a saint. No one was more surprised than I was when I found myself falling in love.

Our first trip together was a weekend in Florida, where Todd had arranged a surprise adventure. He wouldn't tell me where we were going, he just promised I would love it and we'd have a fantastic time. I was excited and very intrigued, picturing a day trip to Key West, or scuba diving, or maybe even a beautiful, magical afternoon of swimming with dolphins.

Imagine my chagrin when I stepped out of the car in my glistening new silver bikini to discover we'd arrived at our muddy destination for our private kayaking eco-tour of the Everglades. Our guide was nearby, unloading kayaks from a truck.

"Excuse me," I said, "but are there alligators in this water?"

He was so casual about it he didn't even bother to stop what he was doing. "Oh, yes, ma'am, thousands of them."

Dear God. "Do you have a gun?"

He stopped working just long enough to glance back at me over his shoulder and shake his head. "Won't need one, ma'am."

If that was meant to be confidence-inspiring, it failed miserably. I was petrified. I wanted nothing more than to grab Todd and yell, "Get me out of here!" But he was excited about this, and he'd gone out of his way to arrange what he thought would be a thrilling surprise for me. The least I could do was try.

So off we went in our kayaks that might as well have been made of tissue paper as far as I was concerned. And sure enough, our guide was right, the Discovery Channel was right, there are a lot of alligators in the Florida Everglades. Judging by the eyes I saw peering from the water all around us, there were approximately a billion of them, and they all looked hungry. It was terrifying.

Somehow, though, after about twenty minutes of not being eaten, I started relaxing a little, which evolved into thinking this adventure wasn't so bad, which evolved into noticing that three hours later, between the kayaking, the nature, the birds, the wildlife, the peace, the quiet, the simplicity, the sense of decompressing and just *being*, not to mention being *with* someone who was so stimulating and so compelling, I was completely enthralled. It wasn't an adventure I'd ever thought of doing or even wanted to do before, but it was incredible, and one of the first times since Rob died that I felt truly in the moment, and *alive*. I couldn't wait to bring my kids here.

I called Chloe the minute I got home and told her all about it.

"You and Alex will *love* it!" I told her.

There was a brief silence. Then she blasted me.

"So let me get this straight," she fumed. "I'm supposed to be happy to hear that you spent three hours paddling around with alligators. What's next, Mom? Skydiving? Bungee jumping? Mountain climbing? Swimming with sharks? I would really appreciate it, and I'm sure Alex would too, if from now on you don't engage in any leisure activities that involve a serious risk of death. I hate to remind you, but *you're the only parent we've got left!*"

I felt awful. I apologized and promised that I would never, ever again take any unnecessary chances with my life. We were friends again by the time we hung up, but it still shook me up. I didn't get much sleep that night.

Since the day Alex was born, I've thought more times than I can count that if it weren't for my children, I wouldn't be afraid of death. Like everyone else, I'm not especially looking forward to it, but I kind of accepted the inevitability of it until I became a mother. Then the thought of leaving my children without their mom became frightening to me, tempered a little by the fact that at least they'd still have their dad. But now . . .

"The only parent we have left."

Chloe was right. No more unnecessary risks. Never, ever again.

CHAPTER ELEVEN

S INCE ROB TOOK HIS LIFE, THE ONLY THING ON THIS EARTH that terrifies me more than the idea of dying before my time is the idea of losing one of my children. How anyone survives the loss of a child I can't begin to imagine.

I talked to two women whose children had died by suicide. They generously, openly told me all about what they'd been through, and I still can't imagine it.

Janie Lopez was sitting with one of her oldest friends along the Brooklyn Promenade one quiet afternoon, telling her about the phone conversation she'd had four days earlier with her twenty-year-old son, Sam. He sounded positive, talking about his upcoming classes at Colorado College, his girlfriend, his campus groundskeeping job, just life in general and how well it seemed to be going. It was the most upbeat conversation she'd had with him in a while. Janie and her husband, Tony, were cautiously optimistic that maybe he'd turned a corner. He must be taking his mood stabilizer.

Janie and Tony's first son, Matt, was five years old when Sam came along. Sam was Janie's mini-me. He even looked like her. She's very social and loves bringing people together;

and Sam could be great with everybody, the first to be-friend new kids at school and make them feel welcome and not alone. She took him to a psychologist when he was three years old about some "stuff" he was going through. At the end of the session the psychologist commented to her, "Isn't it wonderful that you get a chance to re-raise your-self?" From the very beginning, Janie "got" him at his core, the boy he was and the man he could become, under the psychological issues that started developing in his early teens, some of which he skillfully hid from her. Much of the time he acted perfectly normal. She once told him, "If you decide you want to become a professional poker player, I'll back you 100 percent—you've got the best poker face I've ever seen in my life."

Sam was an extremely bright student and a critical thinker at a young age, and drawn to anger and darkness. His literary tastes tended toward iconoclasts like Jack Kerouac and David Foster Wallace, authors whose themes often included drugs, promiscuity, rebellion, depression, despair, and suicide; and he was particularly fascinated with German philosophers. As Janie asked rhetorically when we talked, "Does it get any darker than German philoso-phers?"

It was easy for Janie to write off a lot of Sam's high school behavior as typical teenage angst—not wanting to deal with things, pushing his parents and his older brother away, shutting himself off in his room, and experimenting with drugs, particularly marijuana and ketamine, which was his favorite. Tony wondered if Sam might be bipolar. Janie thought that was too extreme a suggestion; but when Sam would seem especially dark, angry, or depressed, she'd ask him if he'd like to go to therapy. He always said no, knowing that therapy would uncover his drug use.

Sam successfully graduated from high school and headed off to Colorado College, starting out with a major in comparative literature but changing to philosophy in his second year; and he seemed to be doing well. He was interested in his classes and classmates, and he met and fell in love with a wonderful girlfriend. He always went out of his way to make sure Janie knew that people liked him, because he knew that was important to her. And he enthusiastically met his parents and brother at a family reunion in New Orleans over Christmas break, where their relatives couldn't say enough to Tony and Janie about what great parents they were to have raised sons as fabulous, friendly, and special as Matt and Sam.

A week after the reunion Tony and Janie were at their home in London when they got a call from the dean of students at Colorado College. Sam had had a psychotic break at school, acting so erratically that he'd been taken to the hospital after doing huge quantities of marijuana and a legal, plant-based supplement called Kratom that can have mind-altering effects and produce euphoria. He'd have to be excused for the semester to recover.

They immediately flew to Colorado, picked him up at a treatment center, and took him back to London. They found him a psychiatrist who prescribed medications for him that they made sure he took, and they sent him to Narcotics Anonymous meetings. His girlfriend came to stay with them, which made him happy; and with the help of his meds, therapy, and NA meetings, things started looking up. By the time Sam and his girlfriend left three weeks later, he was excited to get back to Colorado, get a job, make money before the next semester started, and be a grown-up.

So when Janie was sitting with her friend on the Brooklyn Promenade that afternoon, four days after her upbeat phone conversation with her younger son, she had every reason to believe that maybe the worst was over for him. She had no way of knowing that after returning to Colorado, Sam had stopped taking his meds, stopped going to therapy, and given up on his NA meetings.

Janie's phone rang, interrupting her talk with her friend and changing the rest of her life.

It was Sam's girlfriend, so hysterical that Janie could barely understand her. She and Sam had breakfast together the previous morning before he left for his groundskeeping job. They had plans for after work, but he never came home. Instead, he drove five hours to Taos, New Mexico, and wrote an e-mail to his best friend in London, who, because of the seven-hour time difference, had only just read it and immediately called Sam's girlfriend.

The e-mail said, in essence, "By the time you get this, I will have killed myself by jumping off the Rio Grande Gorge Bridge. I'm really sorry to do this to you, but I think you're the only one who can handle it. I love my mom, I love my dad, I love my brother, I love my girlfriend and my friends, and I know they love me. I've had an amazing life, I just can't deal with this despair anymore."

"I called the sheriff in Taos, but he won't tell me anything since I'm not family. You need to call him," the girlfriend frantically told Janie. In the meantime, it turned out, Sam's friend in London had printed out the e-mail and taken it to Tony; so Janie and Tony were both calling Taos at exactly the same time.

"Is he dead?" Janie asked the sheriff.

"I'm sorry to tell you, but yes, he is."

Janie described it to me as a scene in a bad movie—there she was, in the middle of the Promenade, freaking out and screaming at the top of her lungs, while her friend held her and promised, "I will not leave you until Tony gets home."

She didn't. In fact, she called Janie's best friends, and they all gathered at Janie and Tony's house in New Jersey and stayed right by her side until Tony arrived from London. Janie was in so much shock that she couldn't think clearly, let alone take in the horrifying reality that Sam was gone. She remembers the awful process of notifying people, and people coming and going, and feeling as if she were underwater and watching it from a thousand miles away. She remembers Tony gently saying to her mother, "We have to tell you something," and her mother shrieking back, "No! I don't want to know! Don't tell me! I don't want to know!" She remembers moments when she was sure a part of her had died along with Sam, and other moments when she'd think that, because both her sons had traveled all over the world and she'd go weeks sometimes without seeing them, the fact that he wasn't there didn't mean this wasn't some terrible misunderstanding and he wasn't really gone at all.

Janie and Tony made the surreal trip to Albuquerque three days later. Their son Matt, an archaeologist who'd just started a job in Montana, had to tell his new employers, "I have to go, my brother died," and he met them in New Mexico to help with the ugly, unavoidable post-death arrangements. Janie's first thought on seeing him was how much it meant to her that the three of them were together. Her second thought, immediately after the first, was the sudden, heartbreaking realization that Matt was an only child now, and that when she and Tony are gone, he'll be all alone in the world.

Janie was and is a very big believer in the value of therapy. She'd been through a horrific depression twenty years earlier; and, as she told me, "I wasn't about to go back into that hole again. It will destroy my life, my marriage, and my family. I will not go there." She immediately found a therapist and started going twice a week, and every day she made herself get out of bed, take a shower, put on her makeup, and go out with friends. People would say, "You're so brave," and she'd reply, "I don't know how else to do this. If there's another option, please tell me what it is, because I might find it a lot more appealing."

A memorial service for Sam was arranged at Colorado College—the school chaplain's idea, not Janie and Tony's. A couple of their relatives announced it on Facebook and added something about joining the family "to say good-bye." Janie hit the roof. "I am *not* saying good-bye!" she told them. "This is about honoring my son! I will *not* say good-bye to him!"

She wished so much that Sam could have been there to hear his schoolmates talk about how much they loved him and what a difference he made in their lives—how alone they were feeling when they first arrived on campus until Sam went out of his way to make friends with them; how he brought everyone together and always found a way to let them know they were going to be okay; how funny and deep and interesting conversations with him were; and how, even though some of them had only known him for a short time, they'd never forget him.

Janie wrote her own exquisite tribute to her son for the memorial service that she shared with me:

Some people are born into this world with an old soul. Some people can't wait to grow up and experience everything the world has to offer. Some people feel so deeply that the pain becomes too much. Some people feel the city can't hold them and the big sky is not big enough. Some people taunt death and death takes up the challenge and wins.

Samson had a large flame within himself, and he had the power to ignite that flame within others, but didn't trust himself with the power that it contained.

I wish I could have shown him how special he was. I wish he could have heard what others said about how special he was. I wish he could have seen how my heart would burst with love for him. I wish I could have healed his pain, but I would have had to see it first. I would give anything to give him one more hug, one more kiss, one more time to look into his beautiful face.

My Brooklyn baby
My New Jersey boy
My London lad
My mountain man
My beautiful, brilliant Samson

I love you today, tomorrow, forever . . .

It still amazes me that when I talked to Janie, it hadn't quite been two months since Sam took his life. She was still raw and reeling, and beautifully open with me so incredibly early in her healing. One of her biggest fears was that she'll become bitter, particularly as she watches everyone else's kids heading off to college, getting married, having children, and living long, full lives, while her son ended his story and closed the book at only twenty years old.

I talked to another mother who's much farther along on the long, unspeakable journey of grieving the suicide of her child. It's my heartfelt prayer that her story might bring Janie some comfort and assurance that she's not alone, and that she really can and will survive this.

In early September of 2010, eighteen-year-old Tyler Clementi started his freshman year at Rutgers University.

On September 22, 2010, he shined a national spotlight on the issues of cyberbullying and the ignorant, outrageous bigotry faced by young people in the LGBTQ community when he ended his despair by taking his life at the George Washington Bridge.

At 9:30 that stormy evening, Tyler's parents, Jane and Joe, were watching TV in the Clementi family's New Jersey home when the phone rang. It was the Port Authority Police, asking them to come to their offices in Fort Lee. Something about their son. From the few snippets of information the police shared, Jane and Joe knew something awful had happened, they just had no idea how awful it was.

She and Joe told the Port Authority Police they were on their way and hung up. Jane felt an ice-cold dread in the pit of her stomach and dialed a phone number at Rutgers they'd been given at orientation, a number for parents to call if they had reason to be concerned about their children and needed someone to check on them.

"We just heard from the police," she told the voice on the other end of the line. "You have to find Tyler."

As she and her husband made the fifteen-mile drive through a heavy rainstorm to the Port Authority building, Jane thought back to her long phone conversation with Tyler that morning, their longest conversation since he started school. It was Wednesday. The coming weekend was Parents' Weekend at Rutgers; she, Joe, and their two older sons, James and Brian, were all going, and she and Tyler had plans to make—yes, absolutely, they were on for the football game, and they'd all go to dinner afterward. She'd bring lots of water, cookies, and ramen noodles for him to keep in his dorm room, but what about his bicycle? He'd become a cycling enthusiast a year and a half earlier, and there had been several discussions about whether or not he should take his new, expensive bike when he started school. Should they bring that with them too? There was a pause before he said, "Oh, my bicycle," almost under his breath, and then simply added, "Don't bring it." That afternoon she'd loaded the car with the groceries he asked for. They would stay in the car for weeks.

Between the Port Authority Police and the information they passively received during the hellish days it took to find and positively identify Tyler's body, Jane and Joe managed to piece together the events that preceded their son's disappearance.

On September 19, Tyler had asked his roommate, whose name Jane prefers not to mention, if he could have their room to himself that evening for his date with a male friend. The roommate had researched Tyler online before school started and messaged a high school friend, "Fuck my life/He's gay." He'd also discovered that Tyler was actively participating in a gay chat room and posted a link to one of Tyler's Twitter threads, adding the comment, "Found out my roommate is gay." So the night that Tyler asked his roommate for a few hours of privacy with his date, the roommate, with the help of his webcam, a dormmate's computer, and iChat, secretly streamed Tyler and his male companion having sex. A few minutes after the webcam viewing the roommate tweeted, ". . . I saw him making out with a dude. Yay."

Tyler had a date with the same "dude" on September 21 and had asked for use of their dorm room on that night as well. At around 6:30 that evening the roommate tweeted, "Anyone with iChat, I dare you to video chat me between the hours of 9:30 and 12. Yes, it's happening again."

Tyler saw the tweets. He reported the incident to a resident assistant and two Rutgers officials and formally asked that he be allowed to change rooms and that his roommate be punished. The resident assistant described Tyler as "shaky and uncomfortable" during their meeting; and in the early morning hours of September 22 Tyler posted on the Just Us Boys and Yahoo! message boards that he'd filed a complaint through university authorities and that the resident assistant "seemed to take it seriously."

Tyler's wallet and cell phone were found that same night on the George Washington Bridge.

A few days later, the Middlesex County police started an investigation, and the roommate and the dormmate whose computer was used were asked to leave the campus. By the time Jane, Joe, James, and Brian got home from picking up Tyler's belongings from his dorm room at Rutgers, the press had already started gathering in their front yard; and an international media storm was under way, swarming to cover a story that included everything from cyberbullying to suicide and the LGBTQ community.

Looking back on her precious youngest son, Jane remembers what a happy, energized boy he'd always been, with a warm smile and a good sense of humor, a very social boy who enjoyed people without caring to be the center of attention, a boy who certainly never seemed depressed. Then again, being gay, Tyler had grown up learning to hide a lot of himself. Maybe he'd suffered from depression and learned to hide that too, behind a smile rather than a frown.

Without him, Jane was numb, distraught, lost in a thick fog and the inevitable rabbit hole of what-ifs and I-should-haves. Her usual daily routines came to a complete stop, with nowhere to turn to escape her hollow, aching grief. Her eldest son, James, spoke about Tyler at a candle-light vigil in New Jersey, and Jane went because James was there. She hadn't been able to handle the suicide part of Tyler's death until then. But that night, for the first time, she heard other people's stories of losing a loved one to suicide and learned that parents whose children had taken their own lives seemed to fall into two camps: those who said their child had struggled with depression and self-harming behavior and almost felt this horrible end of the story was a matter of when, not if, it would happen; and others who, like Jane, felt their child's suicide was a terrible situational/reactive event, a permanent solution to a temporary problem.

In December of 2011 Jane and Joe started accepting interview requests from countless magazines and TV news shows. She remembers being asked questions and answering them, without a clue what words were coming out of her mouth. The media had already been organically gathering, and only after Jane and Joe founded the Tyler Clementi Foundation did they begin publicly lending their voices to their son's story. It took a while for Jane and Joe to figure out what the foundation's focus was going to be; but finally it evolved into its current mission, defined on the Tyler Clementi Foundation website:

Our mission is to end online and offline bullying in schools, workplaces, and faith communities.

The Tyler Clementi Foundation was founded by the Clementi family to prevent bullying through inclusion and the assertion of dignity and acceptance as a way to honor the memory of Tyler: a son, a brother, and a friend.

In 2010, Tyler's death became a global news story, highlighting the impact and consequences of bullying, while sparking dialogue amongst parents, teachers and students across the country. His story also linked broader issues impacting youth and families, such as LGBT inequality, safety in schools, youth in crisis, higher education support systems, and cyberbullying.

In 2011, The Tyler Clementi Foundation was born out of the urgent need to address these bullying challenges facing vulnerable populations, especially LGBT communities and other victims of hostile social environments.

Not only do we continue to carry the important message about the suicide risk facing many LGBT youth, who can be three to seven times more at risk for suicide than other youth, but also our message of standing up to bullying speaks universally across all cultures and identities.

Through programs such as #Day1, which provides

free downloadable toolkits customized for different communities, the foundation encourages leadership to create safe spaces where individuals move from being bystanders to Upstanders who embrace diversity.

And then, in February of 2012, again thanks to the widespread media attraction to Tyler's story, Jane and Joe were invited to a gala at the Waldorf Astoria Hotel in New York City hosted by the Human Rights Campaign, the largest LGBTQ civil rights advocacy group and political lobbying organization in the United States. It was one of their first public appearances, very moving and overwhelming—the place was packed; and when Jane and Joe were introduced from the stage, the huge crowd gave them a long, heartfelt standing ovation that touched them to their core. In Tyler's memory, they were being warmly embraced by the LGBTQ community, many of whom became their new good friends. It made Jane so proud, and grateful, and achingly lonely for the son who would have been there if he could have just made it through that one bleak, hopeless moment of despair.

As for the Rutgers students who triggered that moment of despair, the dormmate whose computer was used to spy on Tyler and his male friend entered a plea agreement on May 6, 2011, in exchange for her testimony against the roommate, after a Middlesex County grand jury indicted him on fifteen counts that included invasion of privacy and bias intimidation, New Jersey's form of hate crime legislation. He went on trial on February 24, 2012. Jane and Joe attended every day of the trial, to be Tyler's presence in the courtroom; and they were there on March 16, 2012, when the roommate was convicted on all fifteen counts for his role in the cybercrimes against Tyler and his male friend. He was sentenced to thirty days in jail, three years' probation, three hundred hours of community service, a $10,000 fine, and counseling. His convictions were overturned by a New Jersey appeals court in September of 2016, and he accepted a plea deal a month later.

Jane's response was a simple, straightforward, "In this digital world, we need to teach our youngsters that their actions have consequences, that their words have real power to hurt or to help. They must be encouraged to choose to build people up and not tear them down."

In public, as time passed, Jane got busier and busier, accepting speaking engagements and invitations to sit on panels, working with the Foundation, continuing media interviews, and keeping up with her work schedule as a public health nurse. "'Busy' helps keep me from having too much time to think," she says. "And it always helps to have something outside of yourself to focus on."

Privately, though, this woman who'd never experienced depression in her life seriously considered suicide more than once. After Tyler's death, all she wanted to do was escape. She even had a plan in place, and she came close many times; but at the beginning she just plain didn't have the energy to go through with it, and from then on, her tendency toward indecisiveness would kick in and stop her. When she realized she couldn't bring herself to end her life, she started praying for God to take her.

Then, in 2017, she was diagnosed with breast cancer. She had a decision to make—to get treatment or to refuse it. It was then that she decided she still had work to do. She had a purpose, and an important one. She went ahead with treatment and a mastectomy, put her suicidal ideations behind her, and chose to live again.

Jane has always been a woman of great faith, and her church had been very supportive immediately after Tyler's death. But over the next months and years she started noticing the biased, discriminatory messages from the pulpit that could easily be interpreted as bullying to the LGBTQ youth—the position, for example, that a same-sex civil union is acceptable, but *certainly not* marriage. And when it became apparent to Jane that her church could not and would not be tolerant of the Clementis as a family with gay children, or of her new gay friends, she left. As far as she's concerned, if we could put a stop to religion-based bullying, the LGBTQ youth suicide rate would drop significantly; and her spiritual core, stronger than ever, now includes the caveat "My faith doesn't bully."

Even now, eight years later, she still dreads holidays, particularly Christmas. Tyler's birthday was in December.

He loved everything about that month, including putting up the tree, stringing the outdoor lights, and decorating like crazy. She tried to ignore holidays for the first few years; but finally she made peace with them by celebrating them with her family in new and different ways, with new and different traditions, focused on looking forward, not back.

She's especially grateful for her ongoing therapy and her therapist's clear-headed, well-trained objectivity and validation. Jane believes, and I couldn't agree with her more, that we suicide survivors are often our own worst enemies and harshest critics, constantly questioning everything about our behavior and reactions, and about other people's opinions of how we're grieving. Some people, she felt, thought she was hanging on to her grief for too long and not moving on from it as soon as she should. At the same time, when a friend of hers kept right on going with her busy life after her spouse passed away, people judged her friend for supposedly not grieving enough. In the end, Jane and the rest of us survivors come to realize, at least intellectually, that there's no "right" or "wrong" way to grieve, we just have to do whatever works to get us through our grief, back on our feet and moving forward again.

Jane recently transitioned into a new decade of her life, and it's inspired her to jump-start herself into saying goodbye to her past and committing herself to what she's sure is her destiny, thanks to all she's learned from her youngest son, both the way he lived and the way he died: "I need to make a difference."

I was very emotional after talking to Jane. I'm in awe that she found the strength not only to just keep living but also to do something productive and proactive, and something that honors Tyler's memory. She's helping others, which likely helped her heal and recover (as much as healing and recovering are possible after losing a child). And if she could do it after the horror of what she's been through, surely my children could do it, and *I* could do it too, someday, when I was ready to come out of hiding and speak up, if I just had a clue where to start.

I also found myself grieving for Tyler, this wonderful boy I never had the honor of meeting and getting to know. He'd be twenty-six now, a Rutgers graduate, undoubtedly succeeding at anything he chose to take on, if only, as Jane put it, he hadn't been too young to see his way past opting for a permanent solution to a temporary problem. It wasn't just what Jane shared about him that touched me to my core, it was also a letter her son James wrote to him, that was published in the February 1, 2012, edition of *Out* magazine. It's too beautiful not to share:

I know so many people you had yet to meet that would one day love you almost as much as I do. Even after what you did, I cannot see you as a sad or depressed or lonely kid. To me, you will always be my sweet, tender little brother.

I've heard the story so many times: how you did it, the night you jumped. The first time, and every time I've been told about it, read it in a paper, heard it on TV, or dreamt about it at night, it still confuses me. I know you and I know that is not who you are. And that is never how I will think of you, alone and cold at the end.

You are youth, potential just beginning to unfold. You are blood, my connection to the past, and my hope for the future. You are beauty, fleeting and marvelous. I know there was pain, and I'm sorry for that, but you were joy, too. Your voice, your smile, tiny hands clinging to mine. I will never let go.

CHAPTER TWELVE

Especially when I hear stories like Janie's and Jane's, I feel like the luckiest woman on the planet to have my two healthy, happy, incredible children. I literally thank God for them every day. And as a busy working mom, I grab every opportunity to spend time with them and, whenever possible, take them with me on business trips. So on June 6, 2018, I woke up excited—later that day I was headed to Los Angeles, where I was to sit on a panel with the CEO of the American Heart Association the next afternoon; and Alex and Chloe were coming with me.

I filmed my *Good Morning America* segment and headed to my office for six hours of appointments. Then, the minute my last patient left, I grabbed my purse and my luggage and hurried toward the door to grab a cab and meet my kids at Newark Airport. I'd paused at the front desk to say good-bye to Carole and Ana when we looked up at the office TV to see a "breaking news" alert. At that same moment a text came in from Chloe that read, "Kate Spade committed suicide!" I glanced back at the TV, and sure enough, the breaking news was the suicide of superstar fashion designer Kate Spade, at the age of fifty-five.

Every suicide headline since February 11, 2017, has triggered instant shots of very personal ice-cold numbness for
my children and me; but this one was a real sucker punch,
as I know it was for countless people around the world. I'd
never met Kate Spade, but I admired her as a designer and
a businesswoman. I ached for her and her family, and the
fact that her suicide was all over the media made it hit even
closer to home. She was supposed to have it all, right? Let
the social media speculation begin.

I was at too full a gallop to get to the airport to process
it beyond that oppressive awareness that something very
sad had happened. Alex and Chloe and I didn't mention
it when I caught up with them at the gate, but we hugged
each other even more tightly than usual before getting in
line with the other passengers. We were literally boarding
the plane when I got an e-mail from Morgan Zalkin, one
of the *Good Morning America* senior producers, asking me
to call her. It's a guarantee that a "Can you call me?" e-mail
from any of my *GMA* bosses isn't a casual request for a
catch-up chat; so the kids and I stepped out of line, and I
called Morgan immediately.

"Jen," she said, "we're wondering if you would feel comfortable talking about Kate Spade's suicide on tomorrow's
show."

It caught me completely off guard. I took a deep breath
and told her I'd have to check with Alex and Chloe before
giving her an answer—we're a team, this was very personal,

and any decisions that affect the three of us are *made* by the three of us.

Then I added, "If they're okay with it, the only way I'd be okay with it is if I don't speak as ABC's Chief Medical Correspondent. I can't sit there on camera and pretend this is just another news story for me. I'd have to speak as someone whose family has been affected by suicide."

"Absolutely. And there's no pressure, Jen. Whatever you and your kids decide, we'll understand."

I promised to e-mail from the plane and give her an answer. We hung up, and I quickly explained the situation to my kids.

"I don't have to do this," I assured them.

"Yes, you do," Chloe said.

"Mom, you should definitely do this," Alex chimed in.

They weren't just encouraging me, they were emphatic about it, and it surprised me a little. I picked up my phone again and texted Barbara Fedida for her input. She was in a meeting but responded right away. "Whatever you want, whatever you feel comfortable with," she told me. "Even if you say yes and change your mind in the middle of the night, that's okay. Your voice is very powerful, and I think if it's something you want to do, it could help a lot of people."

It occurred to me for the millionth time—we really are a family at ABC News. How many other employers would be as sensitive and understanding in approaching me about this particular story? I was and am so grateful.

On one hand, it was a little like being asked if I'd mind going naked on live TV the next morning. It had been excruciating enough for my kids and me to make it through the last year and four months of grief, guilt, blame, and shame in private. But for me, a physician, chief medical correspondent for a major network, and women's health expert, the thought of exposing myself to millions of people as someone who'd been completely blindsided by the suicide of my children's father, and by the impact of that suicide on Alex and Chloe and me, was nothing short of terrifying. I worried about people thinking, "Oh, my God, she's a *doctor*, for crying out loud. How could she miss this? Didn't she see the signs?" Or, "How awful was she to cause her ex-husband to kill himself?" Rationally, I knew these fears were ridiculous. There were no signs, unfortunately, and I would never blame anyone for another person's suicide. But if everyone felt that way, there wouldn't be this cruel stigma, would there?

On the other hand, I'd been doing some reading in that year and four months. According to an article called "Suicide and Life-Threatening Behavior," published by the American Association of Suicidology, there are more than 44,000 suicides in the United States every year, and for each of those suicides, it's the Association's estimate that 135 people are affected by it—i.e., approximately 5.5 million U.S. residents are exposed to suicide in a given twelve-month period, 5.5 million people a year, a vast community of suicide survivors trying to sort out the grief, the blame, the guilt, the anger, the what-ifs, and that vague dark cloud of being stigmatized because of it that my kids and I had been through. If I kept on hiding and stayed silent, wouldn't I essentially be turning my back on a chance to help some of those people, and participating in, maybe even condoning, the same stigma that Alex and Chloe and I found so offensive and unfair?

I e-mailed Morgan Zalkin from the plane and said yes.

Then I exchanged a few e-mails with Dr. Simring, filling her in on what was happening and running some ideas past her about what I thought I might say. Speaking from the heart would come naturally. I just wanted to be sure I didn't say anything that might inadvertently hurt or upset anyone. It eased my mind a little when she listened to the comments I'd come up with and said, "Perfect."

Oh, my God. I was going to do this. I was going to do what I'd never imagined doing and come out as a suicide survivor on national television.

The kids and I checked into our hotel in West Hollywood and went out to dinner. By now, I was petrified. I couldn't imagine how I was going to summon the courage to open up about the impact of Rob's suicide on our family in front of millions of people. I knew I still had the option of saying no; but the wheels had already been set in motion, and it was less than twelve hours until airtime. My *GMA* family was counting on me. Alex and Chloe thought it was important, and I couldn't bear the thought of disappointing them. And Barbara Fedida's words kept echoing in my head: "It could help a lot of people." Not if I couldn't get through it. . . .

It had been a while since the three of us had sat down together for a quiet meal without a lot of distractions, and we talked all through dinner. Poor Kate Spade. The pain she must have been in. Her poor husband, a solo parent now, and oh, God, her daughter, only thirteen years old. We didn't have to imagine what they and everyone close to them were going through. We knew. We knew it by heart.

It hadn't even been twenty-four hours since their world had blown apart. Unbelievably, it had been almost a year and four months for us. It seemed like five minutes ago, and a lifetime.

We still had a long way to go, but we'd come so far since Rob's suicide. Our lives were so different now. *We* were so different now, a study in contrasts in so many ways—much stronger, but more fragile and fragmented; more empathetic and compassionate, but less tolerant of drama, pettiness, and bullshit; more appreciative of life, but not quite trusting it, because, in the blink of an eye, just like that, someone we love could be gone. We'd started texting one another every night before we went to sleep, just to say, "I love you," in case, for some reason we couldn't begin to fathom, we'd never get the chance again. Rather than waste time rehashing a past we can't change, and worrying about the future, which hasn't happened yet, we found we'd each started living in the moment, *for* the moment, and making the most of *now* because *now* is really all we've got.

I'd also noticed a gradual change in my relationship with my patients. Since I went into private practice, I've naturally asked patients about their complete health history during our initial consultation. In the list of questions, somewhere between "Do you have asthma?" and "Any history of cancer in your family?" I've always included, "Do you have problems with depression, anxiety, or other psychological issues?" It still shocks me how many new patients say, "I've never had a doctor ask me that before." How is that possible? And why?

Those questions would often lead them to confide in me about some deeply personal issues going on in their lives. I'd listen, and care very much, and give whatever advice I could without crossing the line into psychology and psychiatry, neither of which I'm qualified to practice.

What I'd never done, but had gradually started doing in the last few months without thinking about it, was respond with relevant personal issues I was having, to let them know I wasn't just listening, I could relate. I still wasn't about to compromise Rob's privacy, or personal details about our marriage or our children, nor will I ever. But just admitting I *had* issues was new to me and new to them; and what do you know, it didn't seem to disappoint them in the least that I'm not really perfect and in control twenty-four hours a day. In fact, I found that the more I opened up to them, the more they opened up to me; and the more they opened up to me, the more I was able to help them with their health concerns, and the more I learned.

The first time I clearly remember it happening was with one of my long-time patients, probably a little over a year after Rob's suicide. We were finishing her appointment one morning when she asked, "How *are* you, and how are your kids?" You know how some people ask that and you can tell they're just being polite and hoping for a one-word answer, but other people really want to know? She really wanted to know.

Normally, I would have said something like, "Pretty well, thanks," and left it at that. But this woman has two children, and her husband was killed in the Twin Towers collapse on 9/11. She'd been through her own version of hell. If she couldn't relate, no one could. So instead, I heard myself say, "On paper, the kids and I are doing all right. I just struggle a lot with the fears of being a solo parent. I can't bear the thought of something happening to me and leaving them here alone, with no parent at all."

And what do you know, she didn't snap back, "You struggle? You mean, you're flawed? That's does it, I'm finding another doctor." She just gave me the kindest, most compassionate smile and said, "No one really understands what it's like if they're not a widow or widower. No matter how old your kids are, you never stop parenting them, and when the other parent's gone, you're *it*. A lot of pressure and fear comes along with that."

It was such a comforting moment, for both of us, I think. I know it meant a lot to me that she really did understand, and I was able to do the same for her. Being human for a minute or two beat the hell out of being perfect, that's for sure. The same kind of thing started happening with other patients from time to time, and I swear it's made me a better, more sensitive, more empathetic doctor.

Better also turned out to be a key word for Alex and Chloe as we talked that night. They'd always been good students, but in this past school year they'd excelled, getting better grades than ever before. In fact, they both commented that in many ways their lives were the best they'd ever been, and that *they* were the best they'd ever been—not because their father was gone but because he'd been their father in the first place. They loved him, and they loved knowing he loved them and was proud of them. They weren't about to start letting him down now. They just wished he were here to see how beautifully his efforts were paying off.

They did admit that they were still conflicted about how to navigate socially through the irrevocable reality that their father had killed himself when they're meeting new people. Should they tell them right up front that there's a widely known elephant in the room and get it over with? Or should they get acquainted first and then tell them, so that they're defined by more than the fact that there's been a suicide in their family?

My heart broke to hear my children casually debating how to handle one of the countless repercussions of a tragedy they had to deal with through no fault of their own, and it filled me with pride that they were turning into such amazing, thoughtful adults. I flashed on Kate Spade's daughter again, and ached for her, and prayed for her. She was thirteen years old. She should be thinking about friends, and school, and clothes, and crushes, and dreams. Not this. Not a life without her mother. Not asking, "Why wasn't I enough?" Not suddenly feeling different because of a fatal decision that had nothing to do with her, or wondering how soon she should tell new people what happened to her mom.

"Please, God," I thought as I fell asleep that night, "let me say something on the air tomorrow that will help her, and every other suicide survivor who's going through this nightmare, so at least they'll know they're not alone."

Good Morning America airs live at 7:00 A.M. on the East Coast. That translates to my being camera-ready at 4:00 A.M. on the West Coast. I got up at 2:00 A.M. to meet the car that was picking me up at our hotel in West Hollywood and taking me to the ABC Bureau, a long drive away in Glendale. It gave me time to check the latest updates on the Kate Spade story.

According to the articles I read, she hanged herself with

a scarf in her Manhattan apartment and was found by the housekeeper, who called the police at 10:10 A.M. Her husband, Andrew, had moved out of their home with their daughter weeks earlier, and her ongoing battle with depression had been exacerbated by the fact that Andrew wanted to end their twenty-four-year marriage. She left a note to her daughter, Frances, that read, in part, "This has nothing to do with you. Don't feel guilty. Ask your dad."

Oh, God. It was beyond heartbreaking, and it hit much too close to home. I didn't just picture the whole painful sequence of events, I relived it—the police breaking the news to the surviving spouse, the surviving parent breaking the news to the child, the phone calls, the apartment crowded with friends and family, the flowers, the food, the press, the cruel Internet trolls drawing "obvious" conclusions on lives and a marriage and a death they knew nothing about, the unspeakable, surreal, disorienting confusion and despair . . .

And I was going on the air in a little over an hour, scarlet letter and all, to say for the first time to millions of people, "I'm here to talk about Kate Spade's tragic suicide because my children and I have been through a suicide too."

How could I do this? How could I not?

The news bureau was almost deserted at that hour, but my makeup woman, Veronica, and hair stylist, Linda, were already there waiting for me. I've worked with these two talented women for years when I'm in LA, and it was so comforting to walk into the arms of two friends I knew I could count on to perform what I call a "miracle transformation" on me while I tried to prepare myself for the roughest *Good Morning America* segment of my life.

I could feel myself getting more and more emotional as I sat in the makeup chair. My chest was tightening. My heart was racing. I was beginning to wonder if I'd made a big mistake agreeing to this when my phone signaled an e-mail.

It was from *GMA* executive producer Roxanna Sherwood, a beautiful message thanking me for being willing to talk about such a painful, personal subject. "You're a warrior, bringing a voice to so many who are hiding in the darkness," she said. She went on to promise that if, at any time during the interview, something didn't feel right to me, they'd be watching, they'd take their lead from me, and they'd get me out. "Whatever you want, whatever you need."

In other words, she was reminding me that she and the rest of the crew in the control room know me so well that at the first hint I was starting to lose it, they'd take the camera off of me and end the interview.

So much for wondering if I'd made a mistake. I was still petrified, but all these wonderful people had my back.

Then came a text from another senior producer, a man I call my "work husband," Alberto Orso. "It's amazing what you're doing. Sending hugs and strength." It brought tears to my eyes. I immediately texted back, "Thank you. I just don't want me or us to be attacked again by the haters."

His reply: "No way is that going to happen." It was a sweet, supportive thing to say. Naïve, I thought, but sweet and supportive.

Most *Good Morning America* segments are very tightly produced. We have between ninety seconds and two minutes to convey as much information as possible, and we've alerted everyone in advance what points we want to make.

The Kate Spade segment was very different. It was loosely produced. I hadn't set up any points ahead of time. My segment partner was George Stephanopoulos. He and I had been side by side, on camera, for countless breaking news stories over the years, including the horrific Pulse nightclub shooting in Orlando. On a very minor level, it's a little like sharing a foxhole. We know and trust and respect each other, and I knew I was in great hands with him. His producer, Kirstyn Crawford, e-mailed before we went on the air to say that George was very sensitive to how hard this was going to be for me and wanted to know if I had any last-minute requests, anything I specifically wanted to address or avoid.

I didn't. I was just going to speak from the heart and accept that there was a reasonably good chance that my mind would go blank in the middle of the interview and I'd burst into tears.

Typically, when I do a remote segment from LA, I sit

down in my chair on set, Veronica and Linda take a last look at my hair and makeup and disappear, the New York control room takes over, and I'm sitting there by myself in front of a screen.

That morning I sat down on set, Veronica and Linda took a last look, and then they planted themselves just off camera, no more than a few feet away from me. One of our Los Angeles producers joined them, and I could see the three of them peripherally, silently transmitting to me, "We're right here, and we've got you."

Next thing I knew, I got my cue, and there was George on the screen, looking back at me, making familiar, reassuring eye contact as he began: "Kate Spade's death has shined a light on the difficult issue of suicide, and we're going to continue that conversation with our Chief Medical Correspondent, Dr. Jen Ashton. And Jen, I know this issue hit home for you last year, something you haven't talked about before on the air, and that is the suicide of your ex-husband."

My cue to respond. It was like leaping off a cliff. "Right, George," I said, "and you know, there's so much that we can talk about in terms of prevention, and how complex a disorder suicide is, and how we still don't understand a lot. There is, of course, recovery and treatment for the person who's suffering, but I really wanted to help people understand the second tragedy that happens to the family that's left behind—not just, obviously, thinking about

Kate Spade's young daughter and her husband, but people who are affected by suicide and are really the survivors.

"I'm embarrassed to say, George, that when it hit my family, as a doctor, I didn't know a lot about it, despite the fact that it had affected three of my really close friends. Twenty years ago, I didn't know anyone who was affected by suicide, and now that list is sadly growing.

"It leveled us. It leveled me, my children were sixteen and eighteen at the time, and I was totally unprepared for the physical and emotional trauma that comes in the wake of that."

"I can only imagine how difficult it was, not only for you but for your children as well," George interjected. "I do understand that they okayed your decision to come talk about this. How did you all get through this together?"

"They did okay it, George, and I'm so proud of them for that. You know, the first thing is, within twenty-four hours we were all seated in our therapist's office on a Sunday afternoon. We all went through a lot of therapy, both individually and together, and we're continuing to do that. I've told my children, 'That will be a part of the rest of our lives,' because there is a lot of shame, and blame, and guilt, and anger that affect the people who live through suicide and are affected by it, and we didn't want that to become a secondary tragedy in this.

"My whole focus as I was affected by this tragedy was on keeping myself together for my children, because I certainly never expected to be a solo parent for the rest of my life, and as any parent who's dealing with any crisis knows, your children look to you when they're struggling. So that was, and is, my primary focus."

"And when you think about the lessons that come from this—hard, hard lessons," George said, "one of the most important is destigmatizing mental illness."

"It's so important, George. I always say, 'We should think of this no differently than heart disease or cancer.' And mental illness does not discriminate. My ex-husband was a physician. I'm a physician. For us it came out of the blue. Sometimes there are warning signs. But this affects *everyone*, and having that destigmatization is key so that we can bring awareness in a way that doesn't just happen when this affects a celebrity, and is more proactive than reactive. And sometimes, with mental illness, if you can't see it, people think it's not as serious. But this is not a choice, this is real, and the more we can deal with it the better, and the more lives will be saved."

George's next words were like having him reach through the screen and put his arms around my shoulders. "And I just have to believe that you sharing your story today will help in that effort to completely destigmatize mental illness and suicide. Jen, thanks a lot for sharing this with us."

And then, suddenly, it was over. Three minutes or so that felt like an hour. As soon as I was cleared from the camera, I hugged and thanked my intrepid three-woman moral-support team, who'd stayed right there the whole time. I'd done it, I'd come out of hiding and said what I had to say, and I'd made it through without falling apart. I was crying from relief, release, and exhaustion as I left the studio and climbed into the car.

My cell phone was already blowing up with texts and e-mails. I was so braced to be attacked again that I was almost afraid to look. But when I did, I was completely overwhelmed:

". . . Because she could speak from her life experience to help others, she went there today. With grace, dignity & candor. Thank you!"

"Such an important conversation . . . so incredibly brave of Dr. Ashton sharing her family's story this morning."

"Much respect to Dr. J. Ashton—the battle to destigmatize suicide continues. And let's not only be aware of it when it happens to a celebrity."

"I just wanted to thank you for continuing the conversation about suicide. Most people do not understand the profound impact that mental illness has on the family and in our society as a whole."

"Thank you for your words today at *GMA*. It reached my heart. Please . . . write a book about your experience as a suicide 'survivor.' The only thing that keeps me alive is the amount of pain I'd cause. . . ."

They went on and on and on, by the hundreds. I was blown away—not a single text or e-mail, or even a social media post, was negative. Every one of them was compassionate and grateful; and it stunned me that so many lives had been deeply affected by suicide, that so many people had gone through, and survived, exactly the same "complicated grief," as Dr. Simring called it, mixed with anger, and guilt, and blame, and shame, that Alex, Chloe, and I knew all too well.

The kids were awake when I got back to the hotel, and they were as overwhelmed as I was as the responses kept flooding in. I had my speaking commitment that afternoon to focus on; but that night on the plane we kept going through the growing avalanche of e-mails, texts, and social media comments. Still not a single negative remark. Not one.

"Mom," Alex and Chloe kept saying, "you've got to do more. You've got to speak up about our experience and help all these people who don't have a voice. They need you."

My children know their mother. Their doctor mother, on this earth to heal. They knew exactly what effect the words *they need you* would have on me, especially coming from them.

And then, on Friday, June 8, three days after Kate Spade killed herself, another celebrity suicide hit the news like a bombshell. Charismatic chef, author, and Emmy Award–winning television personality Anthony Bourdain was found hanging by the belt of his bathrobe in his Strasbourg, France, hotel room. It was a stunning loss that resonated around the world, compounded by the incomprehensible reality of two celebrity suicides in the same week.

It seemed like an epidemic of a disease that's indiscriminate, hopelessly final, and impossible to diagnose. Calls to suicide prevention hotlines increased by 25 percent immediately after Anthony Bourdain's death was reported. It was good news that so many vulnerable people were reaching out for help. It was horrible news that so many people were feeling so vulnerable to suicide in the first place.

The press—just doing their job, of course—rarely printed a late-breaking story about Anthony Bourdain's death without mentioning his girlfriend, Asia Argento. And of course Kate Spade's husband, Andrew, was discussed in every article about her. I couldn't bring myself to even glance at social media comments about either one of them. I felt as if I'd already read those comments when Rob killed himself and the comments were about me. Nature abhors a vacuum, after all. When there are questions, there have to be answers; and if there aren't any answers to be found, it's human nature to fill in the blanks rather than leave it at a simple, accurate, "I don't know." Rob was dead, and he shouldn't be, so it must be the fault of the person closest to him—me. Kate Spade? "Obviously" Andrew. Anthony Bourdain? "Obviously" Asia. I ached for both of them.

I also couldn't help glancing at the calendar every day or two and thinking, "It's Day #4 for Andrew and Frances Spade. I remember Day #4 . . . Day #2 for Asia Argento, and Anthony Bourdain's family and his eleven-year-old daughter, Ariane. Oh, God, Day #2 . . ."

According to a suicide prevention organization called SAVE, the suicide rate is rising. It's the second leading cause of death in the world for young people aged fifteen to twenty-four. One in 100,000 children ages ten to fourteen dies by suicide each year. LGBTQ youth are three times more likely to attempt suicide at some point in their lives. The number one cause of suicide is untreated depression, and 80 to 90 percent of people who seek treatment for depression are successfully treated with therapy and/or medication.

I read those statistics over and over again and thought of the hundreds of people who'd reached out to me after my *GMA* appearance when I finally stopped hiding and spoke up as a fellow suicide survivor to the huge heartbreaking, heartbroken community. I needed to do more. I had to do more. It was time for me to stop just speaking to that community and actually become a *part* of that community, an active part.

And so, after a long talk with Alex and Chloe, who were as excited about the possibility of doing more for other suicide survivors as I was, and ready and eager to help, I sat down and started writing this book.

EPILOGUE

I N AUGUST OF 2018 I WAS INVITED TO FLORIDA TO PARTICIPATE
in a Disney conference on Happiness, where I happened
to meet a fellow participant, a remarkable woman named
Monisha Chandanani. She's an intuitive leadership coach
who's worked with thousands of clients around the world,
including many massively successful corporate leaders,
coaching her clients toward lives filled with, in her words,
"purpose, power, play, and positive global impact." As a
physician/science-based thinker, I welcome interactions
with people who think differently than I do. Monisha is
one of those people. I find her spirituality fascinating. It
may not be totally my jam, but it's a world I admittedly
know little about, and I'm intrigued by it.

As luck would have it, Monisha and I found ourselves
in a private, personal conversation between events, and she
shared the *Reader's Digest* condensed version of the journey
that led her to the empowering work she's doing now. As I
was talking to her, I made a conscious decision to tempo-
rarily suspend my physician/scientist perspective and just
go with it for a while. I wanted to hear her theories and her
experiences and hoped they would give a little balance to

my peer-reviewed-data doctor brain. I'm so glad I did—she had a lot of interesting insights to share.

In a way, her journey started fifteen years ago, with a suicide.

Monisha was twenty-three years old when she lost three close friends, one after another, all of them under the age of twenty-five. One died of meningitis. One died in a car crash. The third, a childhood friend since they were ten years old, killed himself. She remembers putting on the same black dress three times, for three funerals in six weeks, and, in her grief, feeling as if the world had been turned on its head and nothing made sense anymore.

A month before that trifecta of losses Monisha had been traveling through Panama when a quiet, relaxing trip to some remote hot springs turned out to be a subtly and notably transformative experience. A light rain was falling when she settled into the first spring. Several minutes later she moved to the second, warmer spring, and as she did, it began to rain harder. She smiled as she noticed the beautiful balance nature was providing between the warm water from the spring and the cool water from the rain, seemingly just for her. When she moved to the third, warmest spring, the rain intensified, keeping the balance. Finally, when the rain ceased, she went to put her feet in the river water nearby. She leaned back against the boulders and the sun emerged, warming the surface of the huge rocks, yet again providing the perfect balance against the cool river water at her feet.

It was all subtle and might easily have escaped her notice if she hadn't been paying attention. But she's always been very introspective and very conscious; and as she processed this seeming ballet between her, the earth, and the sky, she felt a resonant "knowing" that nature was indeed providing this playful dance of warm and cold currents for her. In that moment, she felt a profound "remembering" that there is something much bigger and more powerful than our five senses perceive, that we're not separate from that something bigger, but that rather we're made of it. She'd been given an affirmation that day, and received it, that if we pause and pay attention, we can connect to this life source, that it is ever-present, and, most important, that this source is a benevolent one that wants the very best for us.

That awakening, that seed of faith she felt growing in her, prepared her for the bigger, bolder awakening that happened when her three friends passed on. The intense cascade of sorrow she felt from losing her friends "cracked her open" to the spirit world, a higher consciousness, and created a profound connection to what's beyond this plane of existence. Just as she had a "knowing" at the hot springs that something bigger was orchestrating her experience, here too she had that feeling, that knowing, that remembering. Even through her intense grief, she felt as if she was surrounded by a protective bubble of love and wondered how she ever lived without an awareness of this lifeline of connection to that source that breathes life into us. The veil of separation had lifted, and life was never the same.

She started to have occasional supernatural experiences, like seeing her friend's spirit, separate from her body. She would find little white feathers, like feathers from angels' wings, in her purse or her pocket or other inexplicable places, and she began noticing that people and things she would think about would invariably show up in her life a few days later. She knew she needed to start paying close attention to her inner experience, because it was guiding her to a whole new calling—figuring out the roadway to this enlightened spiritual consciousness so that she could help other seekers find their way to it too.

Over the next few years she became an avid student of yoga, the human brain, acupuncture, Oriental medicine, and meditation, asking countless questions "out there" that would lead her to answers "in here." And those answers have elevated her life and the lives of the thousands of people she's worked with around the world, all because of the legacy her three friends left behind for her.

She's been shown again and again that death isn't really the end at all. It's a natural progression, a rebirth into what is beyond this life, in accordance with one of nature's most basic laws, that contraction leads to expansion. Without the contractions of childbirth, we wouldn't have the expansion of new life. Without contraction and expansion, the heart couldn't send blood throughout the body. And without the contraction of the death of our bodies, our spirits can't be set free to claim their birthright and expand to their eternal lives.

While we're here on this earth, we have the opportunity to evolve into the higher consciousness that illuminates our path; that shows us we are whole and complete beings just as we are, with all the raw materials we need to become our finest selves, if we simply learn how to make the most of them; and that the more in tune we are with that higher consciousness, the more heaven we can experience right here on earth in this chapter of our lives.

The road map to our higher consciousness is a process Monisha calls "See, Love, Choose." SEE is the practice of mindful awareness, rooted in the ability to bear witness to our thoughts, feelings, actions, and emotional addictions. LOVE is the practice of accepting and eventually loving all that we SEE, for once we start to earnestly learn about ourselves, we often find things we don't like. We judge ourselves, instead of accepting our unique, divinely de-signed makeup, which keeps us from accessing the higher states of consciousness that are available to us. Shining the light of love on what is often so hard for us to love about ourselves, our perceived flaws and failures, changes everything, because what we used to hide or reject about ourselves becomes yet another gift, another something to celebrate. And it prepares us for the CHOOSE practice—consciously creating the life we're designed for and helping us fulfill our purpose. It comes from learning to listen within, act from the heart, focus the mind, and allow the benevolent source of life to provide for us. And because we were talking as one suicide survivor to another, Monisha explained how to use her process in that context:

SEE: You've just lost a loved one to suicide. What are you feeling? Grief? Anger? Fear? Shame? You may have been at peace with your loved one, or you may have been in conflict with them. Are you carrying unresolved feelings about your relationship with them? Are you carrying guilt, thinking you "should have" known or done more? What thoughts are running through your mind? It can be a very confusing experience for those of us left behind. The SEE practice encourages you to simply be aware of your experience. Monitor your thoughts and feelings, without trying to hide from them or edit them, by writing them down at the end of each day. Being honest with yourself about how you are processing the death of your loved one is essential, because you can't adequately heal and move forward with purpose in your life until you can truthfully acknowledge where you are now.

LOVE: The LOVE practice is about learning to accept and love yourself for all of who you are—the good, the bad, the pretty, and the ugly. Through the appreciation of our wholeness we begin to truly access our divinely given gifts.

Cultivating a loving relationship with ourselves is a power-ful, lasting, effective way to accomplish it. Sometimes losing a loved one to suicide, especially if it's a close relative, re-veals more of the ugly sides of life and death and possibly the darker sides of you. It's okay. You're not alone in this. The SEE practice will help you identify your unique way of processing your loss; the LOVE practice helps you express and integrate what you're experiencing in a way that brings you into more proper alignment with your wholeness.

Remember that we physically process our emotions, and pain that's unfelt and unexpressed produces suffering. By doing a simple meditative body scan, from the top of your head to the tips of your toes, you can tune into where you're carrying the pain. Once you identify those places in your body and the emotions they're holding, the exercise is to go deeper into each of them, give yourself permis-sion to fully feel whatever comes up for you. Let the emo-tion move through your system so that you don't carry the burden of unprocessed emotions with you. This may look like a cathartic release, moments of silence or anything in between. Whatever it is for you is perfect. Then visualize a healing golden light circling your body, bringing love to those places that are hurting, and those "flaws" in you and the loved one you lost, that have kept you from true self-love and heartfelt forgiveness, and sealing the wounds. Through this process the body becomes a tool for track-ing and caring for your emotional wounds; for embracing, rather than hating and hiding, the parts of you that are simply part of your own unique, perfect design; and for peacefully resolving the parts of your loved one that have kept you from finding joy and empowerment in your memories of them.

CHOOSE: Now that you've SEEN and LOVED your way to wholeness again, you're in a clean and clear space to begin listening to your inner guidance. Your intuitive voice is a powerful one. When it speaks, listen and act. Its communication comes from the heart. When we focus the mind to the wisdom of the heart, we find ourselves in an extraordinary place, living our purpose and enjoying the ride. You've lost a loved one to suicide, a devastating event that can take years, decades, and lifetimes to recover from. If that's the case, no judgment. And if you choose, when you're ready, you can let your heart open again and you may find that it's even stronger and more expansive than before.

A practice to support this is to take a few moments each morning, right when you wake, before you hop out of bed to start your day, and visualize something amazing happening to you, or someone, or something that you care for. This simple practice taps you into the field of goodness that's here for us all. Remember, that which created you and all that exists—call it God, the Creator, the Source, the Universe, Consciousness, all names are welcome—wants you to thrive. When you CHOOSE to focus your energy in this way, you're matching the desires that Creation itself has for you. YES! As you connect, it will respond to you. Then let go of any expectation of what you visualized occurring, simply enjoy the moments in your mind, breathe that joy into your body, and go about your day. This exercise is designed to train your mind and body to anticipate well-being and delight in your life. In time, you may just see the difference.

Monisha didn't just create her See, Love, Choose philosophy; she lives it every day. She could easily have looked at losing three close friends in six weeks as the deepest tragedy of her life. Instead, she looks at it as the greatest gift she's ever been given, a gift she's shared with thousands of people around the world through her work, her purpose, as an intuitive leadership coach. She sees those friends as angels—they came, they lived, they loved, and they accepted, and the timing of their passing was perfectly designed. They lit a beautiful path for her, and for many, and she gets to follow each step of it because of their service, a service she feels grateful and privileged to carry on.

Like Monisha, I don't believe in coincidences. I "happened" to meet her at a time when I was particularly struggling with putting the shattered fragments of myself back together. I was hoping that maybe, in the process, I could eliminate the imperfect parts of me. Learning to love and accept them never occurred to me as an option. Monisha gave me a great analogy:

Let's say you break a plate. (Not that I've ever done such a thing, I've just heard that it happens.) You need that plate, and you have no choice but to glue it back together; but there's a part of the pattern you've never liked, so you decide maybe this is a great time to get rid of that part. Well, you can try. Obviously, though, if you leave out that part you don't like, you're never going to end up with a whole plate, and anything less than a whole plate is as useless as no plate at all.

I can easily picture that, and it makes sense to me. I've still got work to do on my personal version of reconstructing myself, but I'm getting there, flaws and all. I'm very aware that I'm not who I used to be. Rob's suicide put an end to my perfection myth, and to my aversion to vulnerability. What I've learned about perfection and vulnerability is that by striving for nothing but perfection, you actually miss out on a lot—a lot of opportunity for growth, a lot of real living, a lot of community. It's like seeing someone only when they're wearing makeup. You never get to know and appreciate the natural person.

I've also learned that by accepting my flaws and vulnerability, I've become more understanding of the flaws and vulnerability in other people. And by living the pain and hurt and sadness, I'm even more grateful for the happiness and joy in life.

I'd already started to FEEL this process, but talking to Monisha made me aware, and helped me articulate, that

I'd actually glued the ugly pieces of the plate back in place. Now, rather than wanting to throw them out, I'd accepted them. Now, in order to put myself back together, I'd had no choice but to include all the imperfect pieces. I'd registered it as being more sensitive and vulnerable, but Monisha framed it a little more positively—it was the LOVE part that I'd gone through without even realizing it. I wasn't trying to hide all those ugly and imperfect pieces anymore. I needed to accept them and use them to be functional and whole again.

The sadness and loss and grief will always be there. They're part of the shattered pieces that I've glued back together. I see them there. I'm learning to love those pieces, because they deserve to be there, and I'm choosing how to move forward with them as a part of me. See, Love, Choose.

In fact, when Dr. Simring and I first started exploring my vulnerability issues, she was wise enough to point out something I would never have come up with on my own. She'd spent a lot of time with Rob when he and I were going through marriage counseling together, and she got to know pretty well the man who preferred to keep his life as superficial as possible, who wasn't really kidding when he said, "All I need to be happy are my books and my dogs." So it really struck a chord in me when she pointed out during one of my early "reconstruction" sessions, "By the way, one reason Rob killed himself is because he was never comfortable with facing his own vulnerability."

Okay. Point taken. Enough said. Vulnerability can be a lot healthier than the alternative. Weakness? Join the club. And imperfection is nothing to be ashamed of. See, Love, Choose. In fact, go right ahead and say, out loud if you feel like it, "I get it that I'm not perfect, that I can't be perfect, and that it's okay, because it has to be."

One of my biggest imperfections I'll step up and own, and may always struggle with on a purely irrational, emotional level, is that I feel as if I failed as a mother by failing to accomplish every mother's most fundamental responsibility—to protect my children from pain. When their father took his life, I couldn't shield them from their devastating grief and all the blame, shame, anger, and guilt that came with it. I would have taken it all on myself if I could have, but obviously that wasn't possible. I couldn't make it okay. I couldn't fix it. I still can't, especially on those milestone days and events when Rob's not there. I doubt that I'll ever be completely free of those occasional twinges of sadness over letting them down when they need me most.

I keep trying to remember something a patient of mine, a seventy-five-year-old woman with a PhD in education, said to me shortly after Rob's death: "Life is not about avoiding pain. Life is about experiencing pain, processing it, learning from it, and living through it."

That's true, of course. Logically I know my children can't live pain-free lives, I know I can't protect them from pain, and I know they don't expect me to. In fact, Alex and I had a conversation just a few nights ago about their expectations. He and Chloe had been talking about how much they missed their father and the unique, irreplaceable connections they each had with him. And they knew it had to be tough for me, juggling two full-time careers, and the travel involved, and a personal life, and, and, and, with no backup when I'm not available.

"The reality," Alex said, "is that you can't do the things Dad did. . . ."

My heart dropped into my stomach. I felt physically ill, and I had to fight an impulse to throw my arms around him and say, "But I'm really trying! If I'm failing at it, tell me how, so I can fix it!"

Thank God I kept my mouth shut and let him finish.

". . . But the thing is, we wouldn't want you to. Because if you tried to be more like Dad, it would make you less like Mom."

My heart lifted again. I'll always remember that as one of the sweetest things anyone ever said to me. As for him and Chloe going through occasional bouts of profound sadness and loneliness about their father, I know it happens. Of course it happens. And I know they talk to each other about it and leave me out of it so they won't feel as if they're putting one more thing on me while I'm still healing too, from losing my husband of twenty years and my coparenting partner.

I assured Alex that there's nothing he and Chloe can't talk to me about, anytime they need or want to; and I launched into a brief series of reminders of how wonderfully they're doing, what brilliant lives they have to look forward to, how proud I am of them . . . until Alex interrupted me, smiling a little, inspired by the three summers he'd spent during high school working as a counselor at a camp for children with severe special needs.

"Uh, Mom, you know, when Chloe and I are just feeling really emotional about Dad, saying something rational is no different than telling a child with autism who's in the middle of a temper tantrum, 'You realize your reaction is totally inappropriate.' Would you do that?"

I smiled back. When he's right, he's right. As much as I'd meant everything I told him from the bottom of my heart about being proud of him and his sister, it was no more helpful on a purely emotional level than if I'd given him an affectionate little punch in the arm and said, "Come on, turn that frown upside down." And because he's Alex, he's smart enough to know exactly what to say, exactly when I need to hear it.

I'll never stop being in awe of the way he's continued to step up to the plate as the true man of the family for Chloe and me. He's always there for us and takes care of us in a calm, smart, selfless, responsible way. His emotional strength and resilience are inspiring and comforting at the same time, and he's never wavered from the amazing empathy he expressed for his father from the very beginning of our grief: "Dad had a disease, like cancer, and it killed him. I wouldn't be angry with someone who died of cancer, so how can I be angry with him?"

Alex has always been scary smart. Rob and I said to him more than once, "We used to feel reasonably intelligent before you came along. Now we feel hopelessly inferior." He'd already placed out of a year of math credits when he started college at Columbia, and he could have graduated in three years instead of four; but he decided to be more leisurely about it so he can graduate with his friends. He would always talk to Rob about his classes, and I've made it clear to him that he's more than welcome to talk to me about them. As he told me recently, though, "Mom, even when Dad was alive, do you really think he understood what my math courses are about when he asked about them? I told him anyway, but seriously, he didn't get it, and neither would you, so don't worry about it."

He's exactly right. I don't even understand the course titles. He told Evan and me recently that he's taking something called "Discrete Math." Evan asked the obvious question, "Is there such a thing as *In*discrete Math?" Alex started to explain it to us, but after about three words, we were totally lost. Thankfully, Alex didn't expect us not to be, and he gave us points for trying.

He plans to proceed from college to business school and get his MBA. Then he'll pursue his dream job, something in biotechnology or the health care business from a financial angle.

And above all, whatever he does and wherever he goes, he'll always be the finest son and brother I've ever had the privilege of knowing; and I don't doubt for one second that Rob *is*, not *would be*, as proud to be Alex Ashton's parent as I am.

It was very deliberate that Chloe is only seventeen months younger than Alex—with Rob's cooperation, I wanted to re-create with my children the close relationship I have with my brother. And it worked. Alex and Chloe couldn't be closer, and they're each other's number one fans (tied for first place with me, obviously). She'll graduate from Lawrenceville in June of 2019 and has big plans of her own. To dramatically understate it, Alex and I are excited for her.

Chloe's a straight-A student, interested in history, politics, and writing, with plans to go on to law school. She started thinking about college several months ago. I went to Columbia. My parents went to Columbia, and Alex is going to Columbia. The only member of the family who didn't go to Columbia is my brother, Evan, who went to Princeton instead. So Chloe caught me completely off guard when she announced, "I want to go to Harvard."

God knows she was qualified, but the odds of getting into Harvard are about the same as the odds of winning the lottery. I didn't want to discourage her, but I also didn't want her to be disappointed. So, in an earnest effort at my daughter's expectation management, I replied, "So do about forty thousand other people."

She didn't just want to go to Harvard, she wanted to play Division I ice hockey at Harvard for head coach Katey Stone, the winningest coach in the history of Division I women's hockey. Again, I admired her sky-high academic and athletic aspirations, but let's not get crazy. She'd love it at Columbia, and I'd love knowing that, until he graduated, Alex would be there to keep an eye on her.

Chloe, in the meantime, knew exactly what she wanted and kept right on working her ass off, both on and off the ice. And then, one day in late August of 2018, I was at an appointment at my own doctor's office when Chloe Face-Timed me.

"Mom, guess who just called me?!"

I asked, "Who?"

"Lee-J!" she almost screamed into the phone.

She didn't have to tell me who Lee-J was. I already knew, and I burst into joyful, incredulous tears—Lee-J Mira-solo is the assistant coach of Harvard's women's hockey program. It seems she and other Harvard scouts had been watching Chloe play hockey for three years; and they'd been in touch with the Lawrenceville coaches and Paul Vincent, the retired NHL legend who'd coached Chloe at his hockey camp on Cape Cod.

"We're excited to offer you a spot on next year's team,"

Lee-J told her. "The Harvard admissions committee has your application, and it's looking pretty good. We just need to schedule your official visit and your interview."

I raced home from my doctor's appointment, where Chloe was waiting for me. We hugged and jumped around in a circle until we wore ourselves out and then started calling everyone we'd ever met to share the news. My dad took us out to dinner to celebrate; and finally, exhausted from all the excitement, we fell into my bed to go to sleep.

"I can't believe this day," Chloe whispered.

"Me neither," I whispered back. "I'm so proud of you."

We were both quiet for a moment before she added, "I feel like there's someone I forgot to tell."

I didn't say it out loud, but I thought it—"There is. Your dad. But it's okay, he already knows."

As part of her application to Harvard she'd written an essay in which she said she'd made the decision to live in a way that honors her father's spirit. "My mantra has become, 'Be the me he would want me to be.'" And that's exactly what she's done. I promise you, Rob was exploding with pride that night.

A couple of weeks later, after Chloe's interview and official visit, she got an e-mail from the admissions committee. I was at a train station with terrible cell service when she started trying to reach me, so she called Todd, thinking maybe I was with him. Ironically, he got to hear the e-mail before I did: "Dear Chloe, I'm delighted to report that the admissions committee has voted to admit you to the Harvard College class of 2023. We send such an early positive indication only to outstanding applicants."

In the fall of 2019, Chloe Ashton will be starting school at Harvard and playing Division I ice hockey for head coach Katey Stone. I cried the whole night after that first phone call, and I still burst into tears every time I think about it—my precious girl didn't just live through a nightmare, she turned it into an incredible dream and made it happen.

As for me, writing this book has been an extraordinary experience. It was initially intended to be a message of hope and healing for suicide survivors. It turned out to be much more than that for me—very painful to work on, and very therapeutic, an exercise in total honesty without hiding, and an opportunity to get to know the brave, amazing fellow survivors who generously shared their stories, not just for me but for you as well. I'm humbled by them, so grateful, and proud to be one of them.

Please take it from us—you're not alone. We know what you're going through, because we've been there. We know you're going to make it out of the darkness, because we've been on that journey too. Many of us are still finding our way. But in the end, we're all in this together. Together we can help one another heal. Together we can put an end to the mental illness and suicide stigmas that have caused an obscene amount of undeserved pain. Together we can make a difference, in honor of those we loved and lost. They chose to end their lives. We chose to save, live, and cherish ours, and put them to good use.

You're in my thoughts and prayers.

From one survivor to another,
Jen

ACKNOWLEDGMENTS

I COULDN'T BE MORE GRATEFUL TO THE OTHER SUICIDE SURVI-vors who so generously shared their stories. Their time, openness, honesty, and insights were invaluable to this book, and to me personally.

To "Sarah Davies": I'll always be deeply moved by your story, and amazed at the strength and resilience of your spirit. You didn't just refuse to feel sorry for yourself and let yourself and your sons be victims of your mother's suicide, you let it propel you into being the world-class mom you always wished you'd had. I thank you for the inspiration, and for the reminder that no matter how different our stories might be, we suicide survivors have a lot to offer one another if we just come out of hiding and speak up.

To Rabbi David Kirshner: What a joy you are, wise, brave, compassionate, and full of fire, insisting on a life full of love, faith, and, as you would put it, "no bullshit." With proactive people like you leading the charge, I don't doubt for a minute that we really can look forward to a day when the ignorant stigmas against mental illness and suicide are a thing of the past. And with proactive people like you leading the charge, I say, "Sign me up."

To Kim Ruocco: God bless you for the warrior you are, and for the great work you're doing every single day to guide military suicide survivors toward healing. All of us who've been there have a lot to learn from you about turning tragedy into action and filling a need when we see one. I'm proud to know you, and I thank you and every other military family for your service and your sacrifice.

To "Jessie West": You exemplify a life propelled by love where so many people would find anger and resentment, a rare ability to look back on your tragic loss with gratitude rather than regret, and an amazing gift for loving unconditionally while still enforcing healthy boundaries for yourself and your children. Our journeys through this dark grief began on the very same day, for the very same awful reason, with the loss of ex-husbands who made the prefix *ex* mean nothing. Neither of us would have chosen everything we have in common, but I feel blessed that it led me to pick up the phone and find a new friend.

To Melissa Rivers: Your straightforward, no-nonsense approach to such a painful subject was and is so refreshing and so special, and your generosity toward me and my children took my breath away. God bless you for your tireless efforts to help those who are lost in the unique grief of a loved one's suicide find their way back to hope, humanity, and laughter again.

To Carla Fine: Thank you for being so incredibly generous with your time, your heart, and your spirit. What an inspiration you are to all suicide survivors, I'm sure, but most definitely to this one. Your words continue to resonate with me and lift me up, especially in those moments when my optimism is running low and I need a reason to smile.

To "Rebecca Butler": You're an extraordinary young woman with a great future ahead of you. I hate that it was your father's suicide that drew you and Chloe together, but I'm so happy and grateful that you found each other and became friends. You've enriched her life and mine by being just exactly who you are, and we'll always be in the front row with the rest of your wonderful family, cheering you on wherever you go.

To Janie Lopez: I heard your spirit and your strength and your heart. I heard your love for your husband and your son, Matt. I heard your love for Sam and your determination to honor his life rather than focusing on his death. You said you're afraid of becoming bitter, but not for a moment do I believe there's a trace of bitterness in you, just pain and grief and shock that's still settling in. I send you my gratitude, my deepest sympathy, and my promise that there really is a light worth moving toward at the end of this long, dark tunnel.

To Jane Clementi: I stand in awe of how you've experienced the most devastating loss any parent can fathom, the loss of your precious child, and demanded that it enrich you and the world around you rather than let it destroy you. You and your story are going to make a profound, positive difference in the lives of countless members of the LGBTQ community and the community of suicide survivors as well. On their behalf and mine, thank you and bless you for being a part of this book.

To Monisha Chandanani: Your insights have been so helpful to this scientist/physician brain from the moment we met, and I know they'll be helpful to countless other suicide survivors as well. Your voice is strong, confident, and full of faith and hope. It lifts me up every time we talk, and I'm proud and grateful that you've allowed me to share it with so many others who need it as much as I do.

TO MY FAMILY AND FRIENDS . . .

I know we all continue to live with the pain and sadness of Rob's death, and that each of us is processing those emotions differently. I also know that Rob's loss is profound, and he's massively missed by everyone who knew him. While we all go on living in ways that pay tribute to Rob's spirit, I'm deeply grateful for the loving kindness you've shown to Alex, Chloe, and me. Rob was forever trying to help others, and we know he'd be touched by the many ways you've helped us try to heal.

Craig and Art, I will never be able to express how much your kindness to me and love for Alex and Chloe mean to all of us. Through your own grief, you've supported us. We love you for that.

Ana and Carole, after more than thirteen years of working together, it's become crystal clear how much more than colleagues we really are. I will never forget what both of you did for me and my children. You took care of me so that I could continue taking care of my patients, who are clearly *our* patients, in the face of your own grief, since you knew Rob well too. You did all this as friends, as mothers, and as professionals, and it means more to me than you will ever know.

To Michael and Todd, I couldn't have survived this tragedy if it had not been for you both, helping me at different stages along this journey, albeit in obviously different ways. You both seem to understand that on many levels, I will never be the same; and your gentleness and understanding for that has helped me not feel so "damaged." Todd, when I think about why I fell in love with you, it's because, as. the saying goes, "you saw me when I felt invisible."

And Alice, I have no words. When Jinny took her life just six months before Rob, I hurt so much for you, my friend, that I was afraid to even imagine how much pain you were in. When I joined you in this horrible process, our bond, which had already been so long-standing and deep-rooted, became indescribable. That you always know exactly how I may be feeling, and that I have someone as brilliant, as loving, as funny, and as human as you to talk to about surviving suicide is like the treasure of finding someone who speaks the same language. I will always be here for you, as you have been for me; and you, as my former Chief Resident, continue to teach me more than you will ever know. I love you to pieces.

Dr. Sue Simring, you're the most brilliant mental health professional I've ever met. I would never have imagined, when Rob and I walked into your office for couples' therapy, what lay before us. You were there for my children and me within hours of Rob's death, and you've been our constant guiding light through this entire process. You taught me how to be forgiving, with myself and with others, and you've helped me help Alex and Chloe. You helped me become acquainted with my own vulnerability, so that I could "See, Love, and Choose" my way through putting shattered pieces back together. You've literally taught me/us to be fluent in what I call "the language of self." You've shown me/us how to interpret life, events, emotions, and thoughts in an evolved way. And you've introduced a new mantra into our lexicon: "Feelings are not facts." You are at once military four-star general and loving mother/grandmother all wrapped up into one tiny but oh-so-powerful package. You've made me/us smarter and kinder in the most expeditious way. Whether it's referencing sources and theories with your encyclopedic knowledge or simply making us laugh, or stop to take a breath, you've always been there for me/us. I know for sure that we would not be where we are today if it hadn't been for you. You are my rock. "Thank you" will never be enough.

TO MY ABC FAMILY AND FRIENDS . . .

There is no doubt in my mind that I would not be vertical today if it had not been for every single person I'm blessed to work with. When I doubted myself, you believed in me. When I felt weak, you gave me strength. When I felt like a failure, you made me feel like a success. When I felt like I couldn't do anything, you made me feel like I could. You have been kind, loving, understanding, and supportive from day one.

There are too many people to mention, since it would literally include the entire network (even people I've never met in person), but I want to acknowledge Ben Sherwood, James Goldston, Barbara Fedida, Derek Medina, Robin Roberts, George Stephanopoulos, David Muir, JuJu Chang, Amy Robach, Michael Strahan, Paula Faris, Dan Harris, Sara Haines, Michael Corn, Simone Swink, Roxanna Sherwood, Alberto Orso, Sandra Aiken, Morgan Zalkin, Mike Solmsen, Felicia Biberica, Santina Leuci, Eric M. Strauss, Steve Jones and the entire ABC Radio team, Julie Townsend, Kerry Smith, Juanita Townsend, and Lisa Hayes for being so kind.

With just a look, or a hug, I have always felt safe and protected in my recovery process because of the trust I have in working with all of you. You will never know how much this helped me and continues to impact me. I also know that ABC's commitment to destigmatize mental illness and address the impact of suicide is unparalleled, and I am proud to work for and with such dedicated professionals.

TO THE TEAM FOR THIS BOOK . . .

First, to Heidi Krupp and Lisa Sharkey—thank you for encouraging me to find and use my voice to try to help the millions of people who are affected by suicide, and for being patient and understanding of my comfort level while I shared these thoughts and feelings.

Thank you, Matt Harper, for your incredible skills and insights as my editor.

And . . . thank you to Lindsay Harrison, who is now a lifelong friend. Your writing skills are unparalleled, but it is really your skills as a human being that got me. And you "got me" from our first conversation. I'm honored to have worked with you on this magnum opus. We laughed, we cried, we learned. Enough said.

RESOURCES

I F YOU'RE STRUGGLING WITH THE UNIQUE GRIEF OF LOSING A loved one to suicide, you're not alone. Here are just a few of the many organizations who are there to offer real help, compassion, and support:

ChangeDirection.org: To quote their website, "The Change Direction initiative is a collection of concerned citizens, nonprofit leaders, and leaders from the private sector who have come together to change the culture in America about mental health, mental illness, and wellness."

Giveanhour.org: A network of volunteers and skilled professionals trained to respond to both acute and chronic crises in communities throughout the nation.

Taps.org: The Tragedy Assistance Program for Survivors provides active care, resources, and "post-traumatic growth" to families who are grieving from the suicide of a military loved one.

tylerclementi.org: Devoted to ending online and offline bullying among both young people and adults and transforming bystanders into Upstanders through the use of free downloadable toolkits.

ourhouse-grief.org: Providing support services, education, resources, and hope for suicide survivors.

samaritanshope.org/our-services/grief-support-services: Offers free, non-judgmental peer support and fellowship to those who've lost a loved one to suicide.

afsp.org: The American Foundation for Suicide Prevention is a nationwide community dedicated to saving lives, bringing hope to suicide survivors, and taking action against this leading cause of death through research, education, and mental health advocacy.

If you or someone you know is in crisis or emotional distress, there is help. Call the National Suicide Prevention Lifeline at 1-800-273-TALK (8255) for free, confidential, 24/7 emotional support across the United States.